GRAND~PRÉ

HEART OF ACADIE

A.J.B. JOHNSTON & W.P. KERR

Nimbus Publishing Limited
PO Box 9166
Halifax, NS B3K 5M8
(902) 455-4286

Printed and bound in Canada

Design: Min Landry, Wink Design

Société Promotion
Grand-Pré
www.grand-pre.com

In accordance with the style used by The Confederacy of Mainland Mi'kmaq, this book uses the following spellings: "Mi'kmaw" when used as an adjective (regardless of whether the noun it modifies is singular or plural) or when referring to an individual; "Mi'kmaq" when used as a noun to refer to more than one Mi'kmaw person or the nation.
The area now known as Minas is referred to as Les Mines throughout this text. Les Mines was named because of the copper deposits found there. Anglophones called the area Menis, which eventually became Minas.

National Library of Canada Cataloguing in Publication

     Johnston, A. J. B
     Grand-Pré : heart of Acadie / A.J.B. Johnston & W.P. Kerr.
     Includes bibliographical references
     ISBN 1-55109-479-7

1. Grand Pré (N.S.)–History. 2. Acadia–History. 3. Acadians–Expulsion, 1755. 4. Nova Scotia–History–1713-1775. 5. Grand-Pré National Historic Site (N.S.) I. Kerr, W. P., 1954- II. Title.

FC2314.G72J63 2004   971.6'34   C2004-901528-1

Canadä   The Canada Council | Le Conseil des Arts
           for the Arts | du Canada

We acknowledge the financial support of the Government of Canada through the Book Publishing Industry Development Program (BPIDP) and the Canada Council for our publishing activities.

Table of Contents

ACKNOWLEDGEMENTS

The authors want to thank Ronnie-Gilles LeBlanc, Georges Arsenault, Claude DeGrâce, Donna Doucet, Wayne Melanson and Alan Melanson for their input to the text that follows. Their comments and suggestions on an early version of the manuscript greatly helped to move the project along. As well, we wish to extend a special thanks to photographer François Gaudet, and to the Société Promotion Grand-Pré and Parks Canada for their support and encouragement.

The development and integrity of Grand-Pré National Historic Site of Canada are assured thanks to the collaborative efforts of Parks Canada and the Société Promotion Grand-Pré representing the Acadian community.

FOREWORD

It is no easy matter to write a book about Grand-Pré and the Acadians. Many people have expressed their thoughts on the subject over the past 250 years. Now, after several years of research and consultation with Acadian specialists, A.J.B. Johnston and W.P. Kerr have joined with the Société Promotion Grand-Pré to produce a fresh, new book about one of the most controversial episodes of Canada's early history. This book answers a number of fundamental questions about Grand-Pré's early history, the Deportation, and the events that followed. My focus is Grand-Pré, the National Historic Site, and I would like to offer my thoughts about the special place it occupies in the hearts and minds of the Acadians, and the role of the site in society in general.

When I read the first draft of this book, I was reminded of the words of a former head planner with Parks Canada. It was 1983 and I was just settling in as superintendent of Grand-Pré National Historic Site. Steve Sheridan, on a visit to the site, told me that for him Grand-Pré was one of the most significant of all of Canada's historic sites.

It took a few years for me to grasp the truth of those words. My experience at the Fortress of Louisbourg had taught me that the reconstruction of the eighteenth-century fortress as "a moment in time" was the most effective way for Parks Canada to reach visitors who had little knowledge about the period. In time, however, I discovered that the universal appeal of Grand-Pré is the sense of timelessness one feels when visiting it, even though—or perhaps because—there is no attempt at re-creating the past. Attentive visitors to the site are nonetheless able to "feel" the tragedy of the Deportation as though it has just happened.

This was confirmed by Senator Viola Léger at the official opening of the new visitor reception and interpretation centre in September 2003. Senator Léger, the most accomplished Acadian actress of her generation, shared with me her reaction to the multimedia film presentation that is the highlight of the new centre. Her voice ringing with emotion, she said: "Now I finally understand the full significance of Grand-Pré. This is the site of all the Acadians. Everyone, especially in 2004 during the 400th anniversary of Acadie, must see this presentation."

In her 2003 book POSTCARDS FROM ACADIE, folklorist Barbara Le Blanc explains that Grand-Pré helped shape the identity of the Acadian people: "The Grand-Pré site has served as a historical clue, a focal point, a catharsis, a catalyst, and a motivator, both for Acadians and for others. In many Acadian endeavours to direct and control a sense of identity in a changing world, Grand-Pré plays a significant role by serving as a place of heritage commemoration and celebration—of past, present, and future. Grand-Pré symbolizes a universal hope of survival through obstacles, and a dream of group cohesion."

I believe that Grand-Pré belongs to a special family of historic places throughout the world that includes the District Six Museum (South Africa), the Gulag Museum (Russia), Liberation War Museum (Bangladesh), and Lower East Side Tenement Museum (USA). These places awaken peoples' social consciences and help to promote humanitarian principles. Over the years, many Acadians have told me that their visit to Grand-Pré had a profound impact on their life. For some, it meant becoming intimately aware of what it means to be Acadian. For others, it signalled the beginning of a different perspective on life and renewed creative energy.

Some 250 years after the beginning of the Deportation, Grand-Pré welcomes thousands of visitors taking part in the 2004 Congrès mondial acadien, and the 400th anniversary of the founding of Acadie. I sense that there are many memorable chapters in the history of Grand-Pré still to be written.

I want to thank Wayne Kerr and John Johnston for their outstanding work at and for Grand-Pré. Their commitment to excellence will be evident to all those who read this book and who visit Grand-Pré National Historic Site of Canada.

Grand-Pré—once the heart of Acadie…forever in the hearts of Acadians.

Claude DeGrâce
Senior Advisor and Project Manager
Grand-Pré Redevelopment

In wars and other conflicts, civilians are all too often the victims.

This Italian map of 1566 is an early instance of the appearance of Acadie, in this case LARCADIA, on a map.

PAST AND PRESENT

For nearly two and a half centuries beginning in the 1500s, variations of the name Arcadie or Accadie appeared on various European maps of northeastern North America. In the early period, the designation moved around between the 40th to the 46th parallels (between present-day Philadelphia and Cape Breton Island). Later, much more typically, Acadie came to mean the coastal regions of what we know today as northern Maine, southern New Brunswick, and all of mainland Nova Scotia. The event at the centre of this book—the forcible removal of Acadians by New England and British troops beginning in 1755—changed all that. Acadie (or as it is usually spelled in English, Acadia) disappeared from the official maps of the Atlantic region.

Regardless of the official toponymy, however, there is no doubt that there still is an Acadie. Or more precisely, a multitude of Acadies, real and imagined. Ten generations after the Deportation, there are an estimated three million Acadians or people of Acadian descent in Canada, the United States, and France. For some, Acadie encompasses the landscapes and seascapes originally occupied by their ancestors. To those people, mainland Nova Scotia is the heart of old Acadie. For others, Acadie means those regions where Acadians predominate today, like the *péninsule acadienne* in northern New Brunswick, the "French Shore" of St. Marys Bay in Nova Scotia, and Rustico and Mont-Carmel on Prince Edward Island. More poetic souls shy away from precise localization. They prefer open-ended definitions like "an imaginary country." No less an authority than Boutros Boutros-Ghali, when he was Secretary-General of the United Nations, admiringly described Acadie as "a land without borders." Renowned writer Antonine Maillet offered the most inclusive concept one could devise when she declared that "wherever there is an Acadian, there is Acadie."

The idea for this book originated from our work over the past several years on the new exhibits and multimedia presentation for Grand-Pré National Historic Site of Canada. The historical themes explored here flow naturally from the interpretive approaches developed there. We begin this book with differing perspectives on what and where Acadie is to make a simple point: Acadie and Acadian history are as complex as they are rich. Together, these two qualities make for a fascinating field of inquiry. Our intention in writing this book is to fill in some of the gaps in the general public's knowledge about Grand-Pré, the best known of many Acadian historic sites.

Grand-Pré is a powerful place name not just in Canada, but the world over. Place of beauty, place of bounty, place of tragedy, heritage and tourist site: Grand-Pré operates on multiple levels, often simultaneously. Our task in this book is to make sense of Grand-Pré for readers of differing interests and backgrounds. We ask and attempt to answer three basic questions: What was Grand-Pré prior to the Deportation? What happened in and to the village during the late summer and fall of 1755? What happened afterwards; how did the current site of Grand-Pré, the most cherished of all Acadian historic sites, come to be? Along the way, to grasp the significance of Grand-Pré, we touch on a number of topics that relate to Acadian history in many places other than Grand-Pré.

Grand-Pré was initially settled because of, and named after, the vast meadow (*grand pré*) there. Acadians looked at the extensive salt marshes and recognized the untapped agricultural potential. The first settlers arrived in the early 1680s; dyking began soon after. Seventy-five years later, in 1755, when Grand-Pré and the surrounding villages numbered over 2,000, the British administration in Nova Scotia rounded up and deported every Acadian it could. Similar measures were taken in the other Acadian settlements and the policy of deportation continued for eight years. It was the end of old Acadie, and it could have been the end of the Acadians.

Thanks to the strength of the Acadian people of the 1750s and 1760s and the millions of their descendants, the Deportation was not the end of the Acadian story. In fact, it is a story without an end. Today's Acadians are writing new chapters all the time. Nonetheless, the successful rebirth of the Acadians in the aftermath of the Deportation did not take place at Grand-Pré, nor at Port-Royal, Pisiquid, Beaubassin, Cobequid or any of the other major Acadian areas that existed up until 1755. The cold, hard reality is that few Acadians in the twenty-first century reside on or close to the soil where their ancestors once lived. The nightmare and tragedy of the

Opposite: Present-day view of Grand-Pré National Historic Site of Canada

Deportation brought about the wholesale destruction of a long-established way of life for the 12,000 to 14,000 Acadians.

No Acadian family tree was left untouched by the Deportation. The who, what, when, and where differ from family to family; the why does not. We have a great deal more to say about the Deportation later in this book. For now it is sufficient to affirm that the Deportation, capitalized intentionally, has long been a defining event in the history of the Acadian people. Generally speaking, authors equate the eight years of the Deportation with the Great Upheaval, or *Grand Dérangement*. That there were eight years of deportations bears repeating. Far too many think that the Deportation occurred in 1755 and then it was over. But that is not how it happened. The last British attempt at a deportation of Acadians took place in 1762. The mass movement of Acadians, forced and voluntary, did not end even then. There were further migrations and forcible relocations into the early 1800s.

What happened to the Acadians was not unique, nor is it a phenomenon we no longer see—far from it, as we learn from world newscasts on a regular basis. There have been and there continue to be many forced relocations, "ethnic cleansings," and diasporas. Moreover, they occur on every continent. The fates of the Cherokees, Huguenots, Jews, and Kosovars come readily to mind. Sadly, there are many more examples.

For Acadians everywhere, the story of Grand-Pré looms large as a defining episode. It was certainly not the only Acadian community to be uprooted, nor was it even the first. (The Chignecto region has that profoundly sad honour.) Nonetheless, Grand-Pré has long been seen as the symbolic epicentre for the human calamity summarized as the Deportation. Whether or not their ancestors lived in that village, Acadians throughout the world look to Grand-Pré and feel a bond with its victims. The centre of that village, now a historic site, occupies a privileged position in the hearts and minds of all Acadians.

There are also millions of people around the world who have no direct link with the events of 1755, yet who nonetheless have a profound interest in the Acadian tragedy. Some see connections between what happened at Grand-Pré and similar events unfolding in the world today. Others, less so today than a few decades ago, have read Henry Wadsworth Longfellow's *Evangeline, A Tale of Acadie* and recognize Grand-Pré as the setting for that famous literary work. Longfellow's poem instilled in its readers a deep attachment to the place and to the people whose story is depicted.

The Deportation of the Acadians took place along the Atlantic seaboard

Preceding page: One of many interpretations of the tragedy of the Deportation

English artist Jane E. Benham was the first to depict Longfellow's imagined heroine Evangeline. This engraving was one of forty-five illustrations that accompanied the poem in editions published in 1850 in Boston and London.

of Canada and the United States, a region many regard as among the most peaceful and prosperous on earth. That may be a fair assessment today, but it was anything but peaceful then. The events of 1755 and after in Acadie did not happen in isolation from what was happening in other parts of the world. Although the Acadians were a remarkably independent people, they were nevertheless influenced by and vulnerable to policies and actions decided in Halifax, Boston, Louisbourg, Quebec, and across the Atlantic in London or Versailles. In the end, it was a combination of those outside forces that destroyed the Acadians' way of life, at Grand-Pré and elsewhere.

While the Deportation is a crucial part of the Acadian story, it is not the entire story. Acadian history, including that of the Grand-Pré area, goes back well before the events of the summer and fall of 1755. A distinctive Acadian society took root in the 1600s and it grew and changed in the decades that followed. To fully understand the impact that the Deportation had on the Acadians, one must first grasp the nature of the world that existed in Acadie before 1755. It is a tale that takes us from a promising beginning through a striking expansion to an abrupt and tragic end. Well, not a final end. Acadians and their sympathizers were not willing to see Acadie come to a conclusion. Long after 1755, in the early twentieth century, a historic site slowly but steadily came into existence at Grand-Pré. That site touches millions of people the world over.

CHAPTER ONE

ACADIE AND GRAND-PRÉ

*I*N THE BEGINNING
There are two competing explanations as to the origins of the name Acadie. One sees a connection with the language of the Mi'kmaq; the other traces the name to a European source. In the language of the first people of what is now Nova Scotia, many locations end with *ekatie*, which roughly means "place of." Surviving examples include Tracadie and Shubenacadie. Perhaps European mariners heard the Mi'kmaq repeat *ekatie* so often when they were talking about locations around the Maritimes that the newcomers concluded it was the name for the entire region.

The theory that Acadie is European in origin rests on the fact that Giovanni da Verrazzano, a Florentine explorer sailing in the service of the French king, François I, designated a broad swath of the eastern seaboard of North America as Arcadie in 1524. Drawing on classical literature and Greek mythology, which depicted Arcadia as a mythical land of happiness and serenity, Verrazzano gave the idyllic name Arcadia to what was either North Carolina, Virginia, or Maryland. In the years that followed, variations on the name—such as La Cadie, Lacadye, and Acadie—appeared up the coast, eventually settling on what is now northern Maine, southern New Brunswick, and mainland Nova Scotia.

Acadie likely owes its longevity and its widespread application to both sources of inspiration: the Mi'kmaw use of *ekatie* as well as European familiarity with the classical myth of Arcadie. The one reinforced the other.

Re-creation of a Mi'kmaw family travelling by canoe in the era before the arrival of Europeans

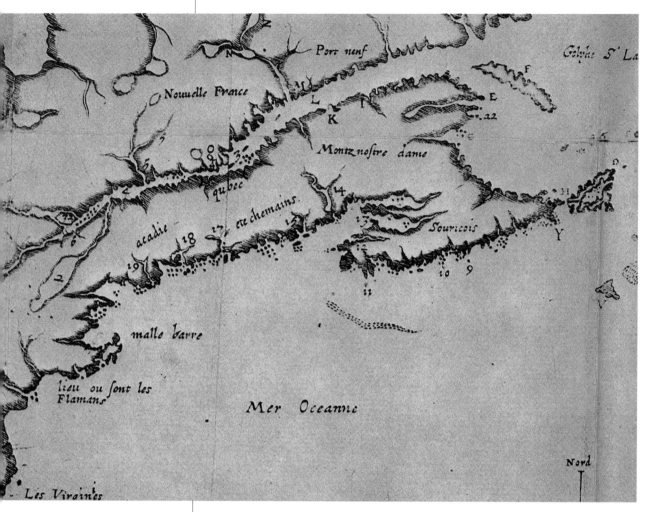

On this detail of a map by Samuel de Champlain, the cartographer placed "Acadie" on what is now Maine.

There was no year-round French presence in the northeastern corner of North America until many years after Verrazzano placed Arcadie on a map of 1524. For decades, French colonial initiatives lay elsewhere. The 1540s witnessed an unsuccessful attempt at settling along the St. Lawrence River; the 1550s, a failed effort at the bay of Rio de Janeiro in Brazil; and the 1560s, two short-lived tries in Florida. Not until 1598 did the French try to settle in the region we know today as Atlantic Canada. Even so, there were countless French and other European mariners sailing in the waters off Canadian shores. Hundreds of Basque, Breton, Norman, Spanish, Portuguese, and English ships could be found off Newfoundland and Nova Scotia, and in the Gulf of St. Lawrence throughout that early period. Thousands of fishers came to harvest the bountiful cod stocks. Some came ashore to get out of bad weather, to obtain water and wood, and to trade for furs with the different aboriginal peoples of the region.

The first French colony along the Atlantic frontier was established on Sable Island, about 90 kilometres off mainland Nova Scotia. Begun in 1598, the settlement lasted until 1603 when 11 survivors (out of an original contingent of 250) returned to France to explain to King Henri IV what had happened.

The next year, 1604, witnessed a new French effort. Pierre Dugua, Sieur de Mons, led a settlement party to St. Croix Island (in the river of the same name that forms part of a border between modern-day Maine and New Brunswick). The colonists spent a deadly winter. Almost half of the group perished. The following summer, 1605, the survivors searched for a better

Samuel de Champlain was a participant in the colonizing ventures at both St. Croix in 1604 and on the shores of Port-Royal the following year. He produced picture-plans of both settlements. This one shows what the complex of buildings looked like on St. Croix Island.

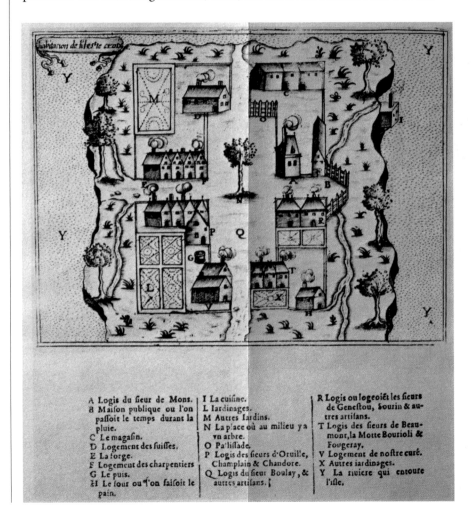

location. They eventually settled on the north shore of what Samuel de Champlain had the year before named Port-Royal (today's Annapolis Basin). In that spot, the French colonists built their habitation. Most of the timber framework was dismantled at St. Croix and shipped to Port-Royal. There would be many deaths at Port-Royal over the winter of 1605/06, but fewer than at St. Croix. The settlers had turned a corner.

The primary reason why the French slowly began to flourish in the region lay with the Mi'kmaq, who included Port-Royal, indeed much of the Maritimes, in their traditional territory, called Mi'kma'ki. The two peoples became friends and trading partners in the early 1600s. When the Sieur de Mons' trading monopoly was revoked in 1607, the French temporarily withdrew from the fledgling colony. When they returned in 1610, they discovered that the Mi'kmaq had looked after the habitation on the shores of Port-Royal. The relationship grew closer when, in the same year, Mi'kmaw leader Membertou adopted the Roman Catholic faith. In the years that followed, most Mi'kmaq embraced Catholicism, deepening further the tie between the two peoples.

The death toll notwithstanding, there is a storybook quality to the early years of French colonization in the Atlantic region: it was here that the settlers established the Order of Good Cheer and that Canada's first play, Marc

...it was here that the settlers established the Order of Good Cheer and that Canada's first play, Marc Lescarbot's Le Théâtre de Neptune *was performed.*

Lescarbot's *Le Théâtre de Neptune* was performed. Like all wonderful stories, however, the venture came to an end. A raiding party from Jamestown, Virginia, looted and burned the habitation at Port-Royal in 1613. The raiders had earlier plundered the Jesuit mission of Saint-Sauveur on Mount Desert Island (today, part of Maine), then burned what remained of Sieur de Mons' settlement on St. Croix Island. The English were determined to prevent the French from settling the territory they claimed belonged to England. This series of events set the stage for the struggle in North America between France and England that was to unfold over the next 150 years.

Following the destruction of the Port-Royal settlement, only a few Frenchmen remained in Acadie. The two most prominent were Charles de Biencourt, who had inherited his father's Port-Royal estate, and Charles de La Tour. They maintained at least a tenuous French presence by carrying on a fur trade at various locations, including La Tour's fort at Cape Sable. By the late 1620s, however, Acadie was to witness the arrival of yet another group with claims to the territory.

Acadian couple in the 1640s.

PUTTING DOWN ROOTS

In 1629, a group of Scottish settlers sailed past the former site of the French habitation on the shores of Port-Royal and built their own fort on the point of land at the confluence of what are now known as the Annapolis and Allain Rivers. This fort was located in the same general area where the French settlers of 1605–1613 had planted fields of wheat, according to a map drawn by Champlain. Vestiges of the Scots's fort form part of today's Fort Anne. The Scots, who continued to call the area Port Royal, stayed only three years in the region. Yet the legacy they left remains today. The Latin charter for the Scottish colony called the territory Nova Scotia, meaning New Scotland. The coat of arms granted to Sir William Alexander by Charles I in 1625 still serves as the province's coat of arms, and its shield was the inspiration for the present-day flag of Nova Scotia.

In 1632, following a treaty signed at Saint-Germain-en-Laye in Europe, Port-Royal was handed back to France. For several years in the 1630s, LaHave (in today's Nova Scotia) was the new principal settlement of the French, with Isaac de Razilly at its head. The colonists busied themselves with fishing, farming, lumbering, and trade. When Razilly died suddenly in 1636, the venture lost its cohesiveness. Not long after, the new leader, Charles de Menou d'Aulnay, and most of the settlers relocated to Port-Royal, establishing themselves where the Scots had placed their fort in 1629. They still retained the name Port-Royal, which had by then been in use for three decades.

It was during the 1630s that the first French families settled in the colony. The focus of the initial colonizing phase of 1605–1613 had been on the fur trade, and involved adult males only. The migration of families from France to Acadie in the 1630s marked a dramatic shift. As of 1650, there were approximately 50 families of European origin in the region, making for a total colonizing population of over 400. Many individuals and some additional families would come in later years. Historian Naomi Griffiths estimates that between 25 and 30 percent of the recorded marriages involved a partner from beyond Acadie. Nonetheless, the initial 50 families laid the foundation for the thousands of Acadians who would make up the population of the region in the 1750s.

A majority of the earliest permanent settlers in Acadie were from the Centre-Ouest region in France (Poitou, Aunis, Saintonge). Yet there were also Basques, Bretons, Normans, Scots, Irish, English, and other Europeans in the population. Other strains in the evolving Acadian population profile came from relationships with aboriginal women; since at least 1605, there had been close ties, including several instances of intermarriage, between French men and Mi'kmaw, Wolastoqiyik (Maliseet), and Abenaki women.

The multiplicity of origins, backgrounds, customs, accents, and other variables combined to form a people who began to see themselves as no longer exactly French but a distinctive new people—*Acadiens* and *Acadiennes*. The separation of identity from the ancestral background appears to have started a generation or two after the first colonists arrived in the 1630s.

Left: Raising homes, barns, and other large projects in Acadie required community-wide involvement. Many villages began as extended family settlements.

Above: Archaeological and historical information on a site excavated in Belleisle, Nova Scotia, suggests that this is how that particular Acadian property looked in the 1720s.

Acadians were active traders, quite different from the isolationist and bucolic impression that some writers and painters have presented. Those who lived in the larger settlements, like Grand-Pré and Beaubassin, sent livestock and produce to French colonies in the region, to New England, and to the British garrisons at Annapolis Royal and Halifax. In return, the Acadians obtained products they could not manufacture themselves.

BEYOND THE CLICHÉS

There is a widespread impression in the twenty-first century that the Acadians of the late 1600s and early 1700s were farm families living in what is now called the Annapolis Valley. That is only part of the story.

Acadians practiced many occupations and lived in a great many locations. Agriculture was certainly the dominant occupation, but, as historian Naomi Griffiths has observed, there were "very few Acadians for whom the sea, with all its moods and mysteries, was totally unknown." There were Acadian fishers, merchants, traders, woodcutters, and people with a range of craft or trade skills (like coopering, milling, and blacksmithing). Even those who farmed did not spend all their time cultivating the land. After all, the climate makes that impossible for a good many months of the year. Those who grew crops also looked after large herds of cattle, sheep, and pigs; they built boats; they harvested fruit from upland orchards; they cut firewood;

and they operated wind and water mills.

Many Acadians became involved in trade, thereby obtaining goods that were otherwise unavailable to them. They struck commercial deals or made barter arrangements with the British administration at Annapolis Royal*, aboriginal peoples, New Englanders, and French from Île Saint-Jean (Prince Edward Island), Île Royale (Cape Breton Island), and from Canada (along the St. Lawrence River). After 1713, when Acadie became Nova Scotia, the British administration grew annoyed with the trade in livestock and foodstuffs that went on between Acadian farmers and the nearby French colonies. In British eyes, it represented trading with a potential enemy.

The occupational variety was matched by the diversity of locations settled. Acadians did not concentrate in urban settlements such as contemporary Quebec or Louisbourg, or in the towns of New England. Instead, they tended to spread out over carefully selected areas, typically beside salt marshes, in loose strings of houses, barns, gardens, mills, and a parish church. One British official described the community at Grand-Pré in 1720 as being "a kind of scattering Town." A visitor from New England in 1731 wrote about Beaubassin in terms of separate clusters of four, five, or six houses set apart by "Small Intervals." The typical Acadian village was made up of large, extended families.

The most populous of the sprawling communities were those that grew up alongside the fertile marshlands along the Baie Française (Bay of Fundy). The earliest sizeable concentration was at Port-Royal (Annapolis Royal). Settlers soon spread out, especially upriver along the Dauphin River (Annapolis River). Beginning in the 1670s, there were several out-migrations from the Port-Royal area. There was a range of motivations for the moves, depending on the time period and the individual situation. Most who moved to new areas were young people eager to start their lives with land of their own. Others wanted to get away from Port-Royal, because it was home to government officials and because it was a military target.

The map on the next page shows the primary areas settled by Acadians. yet there are two important aspects missing from the map. One is the presence of the Mi'kmaq, who lived at or close to some Acadian settlements, and who certainly harvested resources throughout the region. The other is the fact that after 1713, the British viewed most of the area shown as Nova Scotia, which they regarded as their territory, as confirmed by the Treaty of Utrecht in 1713.

---

* In 1710, the British established a garrison at Port-Royal and renamed the place Annapolis Royal, in honour of their reigning monarch, Queen Anne

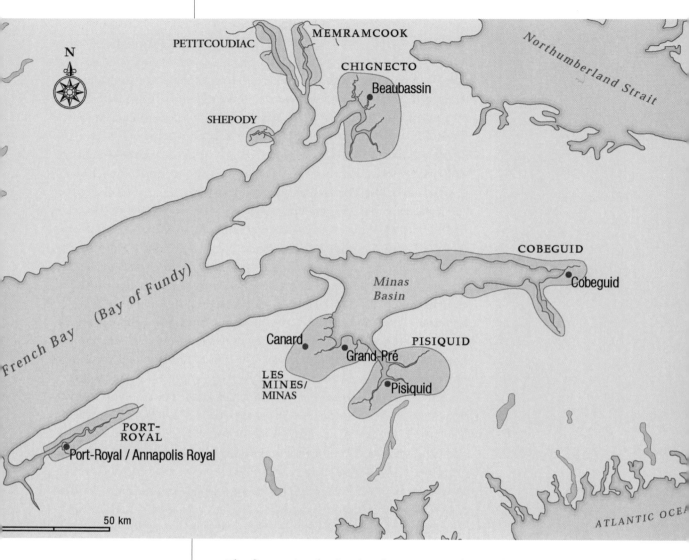

The first major destination for anyone seeking a fresh start away from Port-Royal was the Chignecto region. In that area, beginning in the 1670s and continuing over the next 80 years, Acadians established Beaubassin, Petitcoudiac, Shepody, and other communities.

In the early 1680s, the first Acadians relocated from Port-Royal to Les Mines (along the Minas Basin) where Grand-Pré and Pisiquid (Windsor) would develop. This area would witness massive dyking efforts and come to be known as the "granary of Acadia."

In 1686 and after, Acadians established themselves in sizeable numbers in what is now known as Colchester County, from Masstown to Truro and then along the shore to Old Barns and beyond. Collectively, that district was called Cobequid.

Though Beaubassin, Grand-Pré, Pisiquid, Cobequid, and the area near Port-Royal / Annapolis Royal were the largest Acadian settlements, it is important to recall that there were also Acadian individuals and families living on scattered coves, bays, and rivers throughout the region. Those who resided along the south, eastern, and north shores of mainland Nova Scotia—in places like Cape Sable, LaHave, Chebucto, Chezzetcook, and Tatamagouche —were no less Acadian because they did not make their living on or near the cultivated marshlands along the Bay of Fundy and other bays.

One particularly popular cliché suggests that Acadian society before the Deportation was unchanging—a sort of Brigadoon or Shangri-La. It is true that the Acadia described by American poet Henry Wadsworth Longfellow, the literary land of an imaginary Evangeline, was a place beyond time and change. That, however, was not the real Acadie. The region went through constantly shifting contexts and endured some rough periods. The world that existed in 1680—in terms of demography, economy, politics, and all other spheres of life—differed from what it would be in 1710. It was different again in 1730, and in 1755 and so on. We know all about such changes from our own lives, yet we sometimes forget it when we look at the past.

The swinging pendulum of different governing regimes—from French to British and back again—would be by far the most important political and military development with which the Acadians would have to cope. Unhappily for the people who lived there, the land they occupied was a strategically coveted possession, a borderland between two rival empires as well as the homeland of different aboriginal peoples.

In 1850, English artist Miles Birket Foster offered the first visual representations of what Grand-Pré might have looked like. Foster's interpretation had no historical or archaeological basis. It presented a fanciful image that made Acadie look a lot like idealized rural England.

POPULATION GROWTH

By 1755, there would be an estimated 12,000 to 14,000 Acadians around the region known today as the Maritime Provinces. Most of the growth came from natural increases, not immigration. Moreover, most of the population growth occurred after 1700. The table below reveals how slowly the number of Acadians increased during the second half of the seventeenth century.

This list of communities is not complete; there were Acadians living in small settlements not named on this summary. A census carried out in 1687–88 recorded a total of 48 different villages or settlements. Also, the rapid growth of the Les Mines communities was well under way by 1701. It was around then that the population of the Les Mines/Grand-Pré district surpassed Port-Royal. That area would increase even more dramatically after 1701.

POPULATION OF ACADIE, SELECTED SETTLEMENTS

	1671	1686	1687-88		1693	1701
			French	Native		
Acadie (entirety)	392-500	885–932	877	1119	1009	1134-1450
Port-Royal	340-350	583	456	36	499	456
Grand-Pré/Les Mines		57	110	50	305	487
Beaubassin/Chignecto		127	102	21	119	188
Cape Sable		15	22	24		
St. John River		16	23	294		
Lincourt, etc. (N. B.)			30	357		
LaHave		19	12	48		
Chedabucto		21	51	52		
Cape Breton & St-Pierre			6	129		
Chebuctou (Halifax)			3	33		

A final point concerns the size of the aboriginal population in 1687–88. The number of Mi'kmaq and Wolastoqiyik (Maliseet), as counted or guessed at by French census-takers, was greater than that of French settlers. The Acadians would eventually outnumber the overall aboriginal population in the 1700s—but that is not the whole story: It is important to recall that the French colonists always occupied a relatively small part of the overall territory in the region. Most of Acadie (however defined) remained the homeland of the Mi'kmaq and Wolastoqiyik.

Source: Muriel K. Roy, "Peuplement et croissance démographique en Acadie," in Jean Daigle, ed., *Les Acadiens des Maritimes* (Moncton: Centre d'études acadiennes, 1980), pp. 135–51; and "A Comparison of the Censuses of Acadie the Years 1671, 1686, 1687-8, 1693" in William Inglis Morse, ed., *Acadiensia Nova (1598–1779)* Vol. 1 (London: Bernard Quaritch, 1935), pp. 138–60.

~ *Maintaining the Faith* ~

Missionaries on their way to North America

The Roman Catholic faith was a cornerstone of the Acadian community, at Grand-Pré and throughout the region. It helped to shape their beliefs and customs, and it defined part of their identity. The fact that their aboriginal neighbours, the Mi'kmaq, were also Roman Catholics provided for close ties between the two peoples. Between 1604 and 1755, over 200 priests served as missionaries in Acadie/Nova Scotia. Most belonged to regular orders, such as the Sulpicians, Spiritans, Foreign Missions, Jesuits, Capuchins, and Récollets. The number of secular priests was limited.

While their faith was a comfort to the Acadians, it was a source of anxiety for the British administrators of the colony after 1713. This was an era in which religious adherence was generally more important than language and ethnicity in determining loyalty. Thus, the Protestant officials of Britain and its overseas colonies worried constantly about the depth of loyalty among Roman Catholic subjects within their realm. The reverse was the case in French territories, where the administration worried about non-Catholics. It was largely to address such matters that oaths were introduced. They were a device by which officials, on behalf of a monarch, could reassure themselves that subjects would remain loyal.

THE COMMUNITY AT GRAND-PRÉ

When the most easily-dyked salt marshes in the Port-Royal area had been reclaimed from the sea, the children and grandchildren of the original Acadian families started to look for similar marsh lands elsewhere in the region. The most sought-after areas were those where the potential existed to transform a salt marsh into highly fertile agricultural land by dyking and draining it. Grand-Pré was one such area. The desire for new land, however, was not the only factor in the voluntary migrations away from Port-Royal.

Acadians placed great value on their independence and wanted to distance themselves from the watchful eyes of the reigning French or British administrations. The extent of this independence can be seen in the refusal of Pierre Melanson *dit* La Verdure to cooperate with the French census-takers in 1671. Such spirit was a defining characteristic of many Acadians, though not many shared Melanson's suspicions about the French census-taker, namely the parish priest. The French commandant and later governor of Acadie, Jacques-François Mombeton de Brouillan, commented in 1701 that "the inhabitants, so little accustomed to Domination, live like real republicans. They recognize neither royal authority nor justice." Paul Mascarene, later lieutenant governor of the British administration, made a similar comment in 1720: "they put themselves upon the footing of obeying no Government."

Another contributing factor to the Acadian migrations to the Chignecto, Les Mines, and Cobequid regions was likely a desire to escape, or at least to distance themselves, from the periodic attacks made on Port-Royal by New Englanders, English, and French. The widespread image of Acadie as a peaceable land of plenty has kept many people from realizing just how much of a battleground Acadie was. In the 20-year period between 1690 and 1710, New Englanders launched six separate attacks against Acadie and the Acadians. From 1690 to 1700, the French administration did not feel it was safe to remain at Port-Royal. Instead, they installed themselves along the St. John River where they hoped they could avoid the assaults by New Englanders. Thus it was an understandable human reaction for the Acadians to migrate from Port-Royal. Unfortunately, more remote areas like Beaubassin and Les Mines would also come to witness devastation. One such incident was the expedition of New Englanders that Benjamin Church led against Grand-Pré in 1704.

Settlement in the Les Mines area had begun in the early 1680s, when Pierre Melanson, his wife Marie-Marguerite Mius d'Entremont, and their children relocated from Port-Royal to Grand-Pré. Melanson was from one of the most well-established and prosperous families in Acadie. His brother Charles stayed in the general Port-Royal area, where he and his family lived in the village of Saint-Charles, an area that is now a national historic site called the Melanson Settlement. Over time, Pierre emerged as the seigneurial agent or *procureur fiscal* for other families in the area of Les Mines. He became a "captain of militia" and a recognized leader and local figure of influence and authority.

Around the same time that members of the Melanson family established themselves at Grand-Pré, Pierre Terriot and his wife, Cécile Landry, founded a settlement on the Rivière Saint-Antoine (today's Cornwallis River). Others soon followed and there developed many vibrant Acadian settlements along the banks of the different rivers and creeks that flowed into the Minas Basin—Rivière Sainte-Croix, Rivière de l'Ascension, Rivière Pisiquid (Avon River), Baye de Cobequid (Truro area), Rivière Saint-Antoine, also called Rivière des Habitants (Cornwallis River), Rivière des Gasparots (Gaspereau River), Rivière aux Canards, and Rivière des Vieux Habitants (Habitant

Church's troops destroyed most of the buildings during the 1704 attack.

The Devastation of 1704

An expedition from New England, led by Benjamin Church, destroyed houses and dykes at Grand-Pré in June 1704. The following description of that attack comes from a work published originally in the eighteenth century.

"Next morning, by break of day, Colonel Church ordered all his forces…to run all up, driving the enemy before them; who leaving their town to our forces, but had carried away the best of their goods, which were soon found by our soldiers. The bulk of the enemy happening to lie against our right wing, caused the hottest dispute there. [They] lay behind logs and trees, till our forces…forced them to run.

"Towards night, Colonel Church ordered some of his forces to pull down some of the houses, and others to get logs and make a fortification for his whole army to lodge in, that night; that so they might be together. And just before night [he] ordered some of his men to go see if there were any men in any of the houses in the town; if not, to set them all on fire, which was done; and the whole town seemed to be on fire at once, &c.

"The next morning the Colonel gave orders to his men, to dig down the dams, and let the tide in, to destroy all their corn, and everything that was good.

"In the night [they] embarked on board their whaleboats, landed some of their men, expecting they might meet with some of the enemy mending their dams; which they did. And with their boats went up another branch of the river to another town or village, [and] upon such a surprise, took as many prisoners as they could desire."

Creek). The district of Les Mines became the principal agricultural centre and the granary of Acadie.

By the early 1700s, Grand-Pré was the most populous settlement in the Les Mines area. The village extended along the upland bordering the *grand pré* (large meadow) between today's Wolfville and Hortonville. The drawn-out community included houses, farm buildings, storehouses, windmills, and the parish church of Saint-Charles-des-Mines. During a visit in 1699, the commandant Joseph Robineau de Villebon noted one sawmill and seven or eight grist mills.

Above: Grand-Pré became known as the "granary" of Acadie on account of the production of surplus harvests and livestock that could be traded elsewhere.

Right: Dyke construction required ingenuity to work around the force of some of the highest tides in the world. It also needed the labour of a great many from the entire community. Some historians speculate that the cooperation required to build and maintain the dykes had the beneficial by-product of forging a cohesive solidarity in Acadian communities.

Acadian Dyking

The first instance of using dykes to farm land in Acadie occurred at Port-Royal in the 1630s. The leadership on the initial projects seems to have been provided by Charles de Menou, Sieur d'Aulnay. Some settlers in the colony were from low-lying lands in France, where they had undoubtedly become familiar with the techniques of aboiteau and dyke building.

When the first Acadians migrated to the area around Minas Basin, they soon erected dykes. The many streams and rivers flowing into the basin passed through extensive tidal flats over which the high tides of the Bay of Fundy deposited a rich alluvial soil. Once dyked and desalinated, this area became one of the most fertile on earth. An additional attraction of the Les Mines area was its relatively warm microclimate, which made it more attractive than the Port-Royal area.

TAKING LAND FROM THE SEA

At Grand-Pré, as at Beaubassin, Pisiquid, Cobequid, and at or near Port-Royal/Annapolis Royal, the Acadians established their settlements in such a way as to take advantage of the potentially fertile salt marshes. Since the sea covered the marshes for several hours at a time twice each day, it was a challenge for the Acadians to tap that potential. There was only one way: the marshlands had to be dyked first to keep the sea from flooding the land and then rainwater gradually washed the salt out of the soil. Once that was accomplished, which typically took two to three years, the marshlands provided soil that was far more fertile than anything

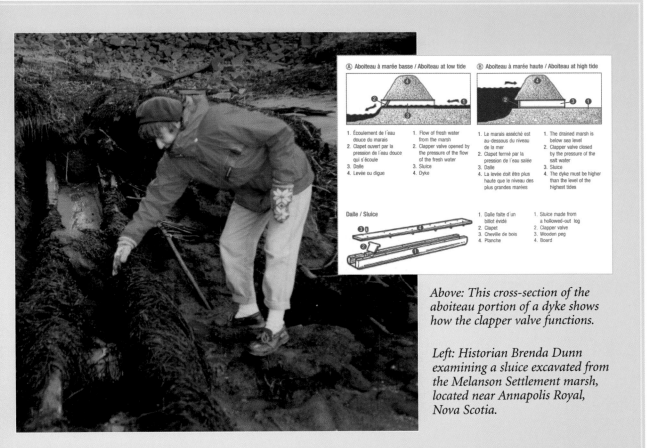

Above: This cross-section of the aboiteau portion of a dyke shows how the clapper valve functions.

Left: Historian Brenda Dunn examining a sluice excavated from the Melanson Settlement marsh, located near Annapolis Royal, Nova Scotia.

The challenge of preventing the tides from flooding the marshes was formidable. Twice each day the sea level rose between 12 and 15 metres, covering a vast area. From nearby hilltops, the Acadians could see that the tidal marsh naturally drained into the different creeks during low tides. Following the natural lay of the land, they devised a sequence for erecting dykes at strategic locations. Central to their method was the earthen dyke, with its ingenious aboiteau or sluice. Once the dyke was in place, a hinged "valve" opened and closed with the ebb and flow of the tide, allowing the fresh water to run off and preventing the seawater from entering.

that could be obtained by cleaning the forest from nearby uplands.

No other people in North America developed agricultural communities based on reclaiming salt marshes in the Acadian manner. Dyking by itself was not an Acadian innovation; it was an ancient technique known to Europeans, Chinese, and possibly others, going back many centuries. The Acadians adapted the approach in a region where the tides were (and still are) among the highest in the world. That required significant engineering know-how. For their achievements, the Acadians became known as the *défricheurs d'eau*—those who reclaim land from the sea.

The first dyke the Acadians built at Grand-Pré was located on the edge of the uplands, about a hundred metres from where the Grand-Pré Memorial Church now stands. Over the years they gradually extended the enclosures, slowly transforming thousands of hectares of tidal marsh into fertile farmland. Between the 1680s and 1755, the Acadians of Grand-Pré literally took from the sea the area of the great meadow.

The Acadians reaped wheat, oats, barley, rye, corn, hemp, hay, and peas on the great meadow. Eyewitnesses said that the fields were "so covered with pods that it could only be believed by seeing." In addition to growing crops, the Acadians raised enormous quantities of livestock, including cattle, sheep, horses, pigs, and poultry.

On the uplands, close to their homes, the Acadians typically planted *potagers*, or kitchen gardens. Those gardens produced an abundance of root crops, cabbages, herbs, and vegetables. Nearby productive orchards grew apples and pears. Flax was another common crop. To embellish their surroundings, and for possible use in dyke construction, the Acadians introduced the French willow. The species has since spread throughout the region, yet is still found in most abundance in areas first settled by the Acadians.

THE NATURE OF ACADIAN SOCIETY

Family connections were the key to the cohesiveness of Acadian society. Family ties influenced settlement patterns and were indispensable to the Acadians' system of farming. Ongoing maintenance of the dykes was critical because if the tides breached the dykes, the meadows would be ruined for a few years, until the salt was once again leached out.

Women fulfilled vital roles in Acadian society. They joined the men in the fields at seeding time and during harvest. The building and maintenance of the dykes appears to have been done by males only, though women helped by bringing food and drink. The care of poultry and the orchards fell primarily to the women. The women and girls also looked after the household, prepared the meals, tended the gardens, milked the cows, and watched over flocks of hens, chickens, and geese. They carded, spun, and wove the wool from sheep, and wove the flax from their fields into cloth. Other clothing was made from bolts of cloth imported from Louisbourg and New England. Some Acadian women were also involved in trading.

The male inhabitants of Grand-Pré and the other Acadian communities turned to the forest for hunting, trapping, and to obtain firewood and lumber. They built homes, sheds, mills, and boats. The Acadians also entered into a fur trade with the Mi'kmaq. There were paths and roads within the larger communities, and some overland trails linking major settled areas. Generally, the Acadians relied on the sea and rivers for transportation, as well as for fishing.

Preceding page: This interpretation of a typical Acadian house interior is based on archaeological and historical information.

Though there was much to work at in Acadie, there were also times to relax. Small and large villages of extended families and friends enjoyed song and dance, and storytelling.

The 1720s, 1730s, and 1740s witnessed a significant growth in the Acadian population. It was also a period in which surplus grain and live-stock were shipped to New England and to the nearby French colonies of Île Royale (Cape Breton Island) and Île Saint-Jean (Prince Edward Island). Though the trade with French settlements brought prosperity to Acadians, British officials regarded it as not just undesirable but illegal. Similarly, when Acadians traded with New England in the period before the British took over the colony (1710–13), the French authorities considered that activity illegal.

Whether French or British, merchants provided goods to the Acadians that were otherwise unavailable. Traders brought cloth, wool (supplementing what local looms produced), hardware, and utensils of British manufacture. Other imported commodities were sugar, molasses, tobacco, and rum from the French West Indies. Archaeological excavations confirm that Acadians had a wide range of imported ceramics and other items. Those objects provide tangible evidence of contacts with places like New England and Louisbourg.

Building a home for newlyweds, braking linen, weaving fabric, butchering livestock, spring planting, fall harvests—these were all opportunities for festive celebrations. Co-operation and support were also there when disaster struck, as when a sea surge or storm damaged a dyke, fire destroyed a home, or an enemy attack brought death and devastation.

Little is known about how the inhabitants spent their spare time. Like many in the 1700s, Acadians occasionally smoked pipes and drank wine, spruce beer, rum, and apple cider. They also played cards, which was a popular pastime of the era. One observer stated that they amused themselves with "rustic song and dance" during long winters. Archaeological excavations have uncovered Jew's harps. Fiddles were undoubtedly a popular instrument as well, for they are mentioned in Louisbourg documentation. In light of the rich musical tradition that forms part of contemporary Acadian culture, there is no doubt that song and dance, and storytelling, formed an important part of Acadian life in the period before 1755.

The Acadian inhabitants of the Les Mines and other districts adopted some habits and practices of the Mi'kmaq. For example, they adopted two modes of transport, travelling on snowshoes through the heavy snows of winter and by canoes along the waterways of summer. Generally speaking, there were close relations between the Acadians and the Mi'kmaq, though that relationship became strained in the 1750s.

CHAPTER TWO

BATTLE FOR EMPIRE, STRUGGLE FOR SURVIVAL

The largest Acadian communities—at Grand-Pré, Pisiquid, Beaubassin, Cobequid, and in the vicinity of Annapolis Royal—grew in size and complexity throughout the 35 years following the British assumption of sovereignty over the region in 1713. Peace and prosperity marked most of the post-Utrecht period, but it was not to continue indefinitely. In the mid-1740s, decision-makers in Great Britain and France rekindled old conflicts. Their competing dreams of power, glory, and territorial advantage led to war. Inevitably, the Acadians living in the strategic borderland of Nova Scotia were drawn into the conflict.

CLASH OF EMPIRES

The main theatre of the War of the Austrian Succession (1740–1748) was in Europe, yet Atlantic Canada saw its share of action. In May 1744, a French expedition out of Louisbourg, commanded by François du Pont Duvivier, easily captured the fishing community at Canso on the Nova Scotia coast close to Cape Breton Island. Canso was one of only two English-speaking and Protestant settlements on the entire Nova Scotia mainland. Soon after, French privateers based at Louisbourg began an aggressive campaign at sea, capturing many English and New England fishing and merchant ships.

The success of the 1745 New England expedition to Louisbourg delighted those who took part, and those who supported it back in Massachusetts and other American colonies. The French were bitterly disappointed to see their formidable fortifications fall to an army of so-called "amateurs," the provincial soldiers of New England. The siege lasted roughly six weeks, and the British naval blockade played a determining role by capturing or scaring off potential French assistance.

With the loss of Canso to the French, the British were left with only one base in the region they called Nova Scotia. That was Annapolis Royal, still referred to by most French and Acadians by its former name of Port-Royal. Twice that summer of 1744, the French, Mi'kmaq, and Wolastoqiyik (Maliseet) attacked Annapolis Royal. Acadians were encouraged to join the campaigns, yet few did. In the end, neither attempt to take Annapolis Royal was successful, though there were moments when the British garrison gave serious thought to surrendering.

The following year, 1745, as the French were once more about to lay siege to Annapolis Royal, an army of provincial soldiers from New England, supported by British warships, stunned the defenders of the French stronghold at Louisbourg. After a six-week siege, the attackers prevailed, and changed the spelling of their acquisition slightly, by dropping an "o", and Louisbourg became Louisburg. It was a major setback for French imperial aspirations on the Atlantic frontier.

Versailles tried to make up for the loss of their stronghold, Louisbourg, the very next year. In 1746, France organized a massive expedition of about 70 ships and 13,000 men, led by the Duc d'Anville, to sail across the Atlantic to re-assert the French presence in the Maritime region. The ambitious intentions, however, were for naught. Delays, incompetence, storms, and illnesses turned the armada led by the Duc d'Anville into a disaster. Despite that setback, a French and Amerindian land force from Canada mounted another siege on Annapolis Royal in 1746, before withdrawing to Beaubassin the same fall. An expeditionary force from New England arrived at Grand-Pré in the autumn to prevent another attack on Annapolis Royal.

A few months later, during the winter, the French and Amerindian force at Beaubassin completely surprised the New Englanders camped at Grand-Pré. Capt. Nicolas-Antoine Coulon de Villiers led an expedition of 250 French soldiers and 50 Amerindian allies on a midwinter trek from Beaubassin to Grand-Pré. They were joined or assisted by a small number of Acadians. Though the French and Amerindian force was greatly outnumbered by the roughly 500 New England soldiers quartered in Acadian houses at Grand-Pré, the attackers enjoyed the element of surprise. In the early morning hours on February 11, in the middle of a snowstorm, the French and Amerindians won a total victory. Known to history as the Battle of Grand-Pré, the encounter left at least 80 New Englanders dead, including their commander, Col. Arthur Noble.

Eyewitness Accounts
1747 Battle of Grand-Pré

"Some of the Inhabitants [of Grand-Pré] about this time began to suggest that [the French would] force our quarters, and intimated that we might expect them in a short time; but the general opinion…was that it was impracticable for a large number of troops to traverse from Chignecto at that season."

    - Charles Morris, English Officer

"After a march of 17 days, more fatigued by the quantity of snow and excessive cold than by the distance, we arrived…at Pisiquid, distant about 7 leagues from Grand-Pré. We passed the night in the houses of the inhabitants after having placed a guard upon the roads to prevent communication, and that the news of our march might not be carried to our enemies…"

    - Pierre La Corne, French Officer

"…about three in the morning the Enemy Attackt us. It Stormed with Snow at that time…They knew all our Quarters & the numbers Station'd in every House…"

    - Charles Morris, English Officer

"We found as they had told us, the houses well guarded, but the sentinels did not discover us until we were within gun range. The night being extremely dark we made a lively attack notwithstanding the fire of the enemies. We forced the houses with axes, and in very little time rendered ourselves masters of them…"

    - Pierre La Corne, French Officer

"…[They] surround[ed] almost every officer's quarters within a few minutes…and after killing the sentries, rushed into many of the houses and destroy[ed] many [men] in their beds, so that before daylight they had killed about 70 and taken upwards of 60 prisoners…"

    - Benjamin Goldthwaite, English Officer:

OUR from yͤ S.E. 75..

REFERENCES.

1 Officers quarters
2 Soldiers barracks
3 Gate way
4 Bastion in wᵗʰ yͤ Magᵉⁿ wᵗ Mine

6 The Hospital
7 The New Church
8 Island la Valiere
9 The River Mesagouche

27

BRITISH INITIATIVES, FRENCH RESPONSE

Britain, France, and the other combatants formally ended the War of the Austrian Succession with the Treaty of Aix-la-Chapelle in 1748. The agreement, however, was more temporary truce than lasting peace.

The British returned Île Saint-Jean and Île Royale to the French, who re-occupied the island colonies in a major way in the summer of 1749. With Louisbourg back in French hands, the British immediately set out to establish their own stronghold. They selected Halifax, known for centuries to the Mi'kmaq as Kjipuktuk (Chibouguetou), as the harbour where they would erect a counterbalance to the Cape Breton fortress. The early 1750s witnessed a series of British movements

Preceding page: The French hoped their fort at Beauséjour was strong enough to allow them to retain control of the west side of the Missaguash River.

Mi'kmaw warrior, about 1745

in different parts of Nova Scotia. The Halifax peninsula and the Dartmouth shore were fortified, as was the Acadian community of Pisiquid, with Fort Edward. The Grand-Pré region received its own small fort and garrison, known as the Vieux Logis.

Meanwhile, in the long-settled Acadian region known as Chignecto, the British built Fort Lawrence. In fact, that fort was constructed on a ridge where the Acadian village of Beaubassin had stood until the inhabitants were convinced and compelled by the French to move and burn their houses. As part of the same process of extending the British presence in the region, Lunenburg was founded in 1753 by foreign Protestants. That initiative is a reminder that religion was then considered more important than ethnicity in determining the loyalty of subjects.

> *…religion was then considered more important than ethnicity in determining the loyalty of subjects.*

In addition to forts and settlements, the British also embarked on a two-tier approach with the Mi'kmaq and the Wolastoqiyik (Maliseet). On the one hand, the administration at Halifax sought to enter into "peace and friendship" treaties, such as the one signed in 1752. On the other hand, the British brought companies of rangers to the colony who were skilled in "forest warfare." This military approach was adopted especially with the Mi'kmaq who did not take part in the treaty process but remained allied with the French. The British paid bounties for Amerindian scalps, as the French did at Louisbourg for British scalps.

The French were not idle while the British were expanding their presence in the region. At Louisbourg, the French doubled their garrison in 1749, then doubled it again in 1755. Simultaneously, the French erected their own new forts and posts in strategic locations like the mouth of the St. John River and on both coasts of the Chignecto isthmus. The most important of the new fortifications was the fort at Beauséjour, atop a ridge on the west side of the Missaguash River. Not far away, on the east side of the river, was Fort Lawrence, atop its own ridge. Clearly, the Chignecto isthmus, where the forts of two empires faced each other in broad daylight, was a strategic zone of high importance. Not surprisingly, when war was to flare again in North America between Britain and France, the sparks would first fly in the Chignecto region. When that happened, in the spring of 1755, the consequences for the Acadians would be devastating.

ACADIANS CAUGHT IN THE MIDDLE

The Acadian communities were aware of and affected by the various French and British moves of 1749 and the early 1750s. Many worried about the looming conflict. Like the Mi'kmaq, the Acadians could see plainly that the founding of Halifax marked the beginning of a new British determination to colonize Nova Scotia with subjects loyal to their crown and their interests.

As storm clouds darkened around them, the Acadians pondered their future. Contrary to a widely held view, the Acadians of this period were not naïve and simple, nor unaware of the difficulties unfolding around them. Acadians had survived for over a century in a colony that had seen more attacks and changes of ownership than had any other in North America. They had withstood storms and bad weather and had overcome natural forces that included some of the highest tides in the world. They accomplished these things by using their wits and a home-grown shrewdness. As the situation developed in the 1750s, most Acadians saw little or no reason to abandon their traditional position of neutrality. To their way of thinking, it had worked as long as anyone could remember. It was the star by which they steered their course.

The Mi'kmaq Give Warning

In 1749 the Mi'kmaq responded to the British settlement at Halifax with a strongly worded letter to Gov. Edward Cornwallis. That letter, reprinted here in part, articulated their concerns—and gave a warning to the British.

"The place where you are, where you are building dwellings, where you are now building a fort, where you want, as it were, to enthrone yourself, this land of which you wish to make yourself now absolute master, this land belongs to me. I have come from it as certainly as the grass, it is the very place of my birth and of my dwelling, this land belongs to me, the Native person, yes I swear, it is God who has given it to be my country for ever…you drive me out; where do you want me to take refuge? You have taken almost all this land in all its extent.

Your residence at Port Royal does not cause me great anger because you see that I have left you there at peace for a long time, but now you force me to speak out by the great theft you have perpetrated against me."

Symbolic representation of Acadians caught in the middle between the British and French empires.

Nonetheless, in order to escape the growing "troubles," almost half of the total Acadian population voluntarily relocated from their home villages on the Nova Scotia mainland to go live in French-controlled territory in the Chignecto region, on Île Saint-Jean and Île Royale. The primary reasons behind the exodus were: the expanding British military presence; intensifying pressure from the French, Mi'kmaq, and British to force the Acadians to support their differing sides; outbreaks of guerilla campaigns; and free rations from the French authorities to induce the Acadians to come to Île Saint-Jean and Île Royale.

UNOFFICIAL WAR, BUT WAR ALL THE SAME

The period of Anglo-French tension finally came to a head in June 1755. Though Britain and France were officially at peace, and would remain so until 1756, actual warfare between the two powers began in the Ohio Valley in 1754. On the sealanes to North America, British squadrons imposed blockades and seized French vessels heading for Louisbourg and Quebec. It

Attack on Beauséjour

In early June 1755, a fleet of 31 British transport warships sailed into the Chignecto Basin carrying nearly 2,000 provincial troops from New England and 270 British regulars. A young British officer, Lt. Col. Robert Monckton, was in command. The besiegers quickly assumed the high ground. Since the attackers outnumbered the French defenders by four to one, they made short work of the place. The French commander, Louis Du Pont Duchambon de Vergor, surrendered on June 16, two weeks after the landing. Vergor knew no relief was coming from either Quebec or Louisbourg. Moreover, the fort had suffered a devastating hit on one of its bombproof casemates, demonstrating the impossibility of holding out for any length of time. The surrender of the French fort on Baie Verte, Fort Gaspareau, was included with the capitulation of Beauséjour.

was a virtual war—all that was missing were the official declarations on both sides.

The hostile atmosphere reached a new level in June 1755 when a military expedition made its way to the Chignecto isthmus. Its objective was to capture the various French forts in the zone, beginning with the one at Beauséjour.

THE PERENNIAL QUESTION

The surrender of the French commander at Beauséjour to Lt.-Col. Monckton began a series of events that would shake the entire Acadian society, including Grand-Pré, to its foundation.

The matter of Acadian neutrality—whether or not they would take the standard oath of loyalty to the British monarch after the 1713 Treaty of Utrecht—was an issue that had troubled Acadians and British administrations for decades.

The British authorities in Halifax, led by acting governor Charles Lawrence, interpreted the participation of 200 to 300 Acadians in the defence of Beauséjour as a sign of complicity on the part of the "neutral" Acadians who lived in the Chignecto region. Lawrence and others dismissed the fact that the French commander declared that he had compelled the Acadians to help defend the fort. The Halifax administration had read reports that most if not all Acadians in that region had sworn oaths of allegiance to the French king. The presence of the 200 to 300 men within the fort at Beauséjour seemed to confirm what they had been hearing.

The matter of Acadian neutrality—whether or not they would take the standard oath of loyalty to the British monarch after the 1713 Treaty of Utrecht—was an issue that had troubled Acadians and British administrations for decades. When the British capital had been at Annapolis Royal, the administrators had been fairly understanding of the predicament in which the Acadians found themselves. They knew the Acadians were being pressured by French, British, and even Mi'kmaq as to where they should lend their support and assistance. After Halifax was founded in 1749, however, and the British erected new forts and settlements, there was a definite hardening of British officials' attitudes toward the Acadians. The new administration was not sympathetic to the plight of the Acadians, nor did it recognize Acadian neutrality in the same light.

The officials who comprised the Nova Scotia Council in 1755 were led by acting governor Charles Lawrence. With the capture of the French forts at Beauséjour and Gaspareau in June 1755, the Council resolved to settle the Acadian question once and for all. Soon after learning of the victory, the officials in Halifax decided that all Acadians in the Chignecto region would be rounded up and deported, regardless of whether they or a member of their family had been active in the defence of Beauséjour. About a month later, on July 28, the Nova Scotia Council would take a decision to remove every Acadian—men, women and children—from the British colony of Nova Scotia, not just from the Chignecto region.

Opposite: The French defenders of the fort at Beauséjour were greatly outnumbered when a large force of British and New England soldiers attacked in June 1755.

Oaths and Sovereignty

The colonial era in what are now the Maritime Provinces of Canada was an often confusing and turbulent period. One gets a hint of the complexity of the era just by looking at the three different names used to identify overlapping portions of the region. What the British called Nova Scotia formed part of what the French and Acadians knew as Acadie, though the British territorial claims extended as far as the Gaspé region. Meanwhile, the Mi'kmaq saw what we now know as mainland Nova Scotia as containing several districts of what they regarded as Mi'kma'ki.

The extracts below reveal the conflicting points of view on whose land it was and where loyalties should lie.

Letter of the Mi'kmaq to the British at Annapolis Royal, 1720.

"We believe that God gave us this land….However we see that you want to drive us from the places where you are living, and you threaten to reduce us to servitude, which is something you should not dream of. We are our own masters, not subordinate to anyone….If we wanted to go to England to live there, what would they say to us, if not to make us leave. For the same reason, we do not want the English living in our land, the land we hold only from God. We will dispute that with all men who want to live here without our consent."

Marquis de la Jonquière, Governor-General of New France, 1751.

"WE DECLARE by the present ordinance that all Acadians who (within eight days of the publication of this) have not taken the oath of fidelity and are not incorporated within the Militia companies which we have created, will be declared rebels to the orders of the King and as such expelled from the lands which they hold. To which end we Order S. Deschaillons de St. Ours, Commandant at Beauséjour… to fulfill this fully and that our intentions shall be known by all, the reading of this ordinance shall be made everywhere where it has need to be."

ACADIAN PETITIONS, JUNE 1755

At the same time as the British and Anglo-American expedition was in the early stages of its assault on the fort at Beauséjour, the Halifax administration issued an order that the Acadians of Les Mines and Pisiquid were to take their guns and pistols to Fort Edward. Within a week, on June 10, twenty-five Acadians of Les Mines, Pisiquid, and River Canard sent a petition to acting governor Charles Lawrence. The document affirmed that the Acadians should be trusted. Specifically, they asked that their rights to move foodstuffs by boat be reinstated and that their confiscated weapons be returned. The authorities in Halifax reacted negatively to some of the phrases and sentiments

Petition of 203 Acadians in the Les Mines, River Canard and neighbouring districts, July 1755.

"...we all take the liberty of representing to His Excellency, and to all inhabitants, that we and our fathers, having taken an oath of fidelity, which has been approved several times in the name of the King, and under the privileges of which we have lived faithful and obedient...we will never prove so fickle as to take an oath which changes, ever so little, the conditions and privileges obtained for us by our sovereigns and our fathers in the past.

"And as we are well aware that the king, our master, loves and protects only constant, faithful, and free subjects, and as it is only by virtue of his kindness, and of the fidelity which we have always preserved towards his majesty, that he has granted to us, and that he still continues to grant to us, the entire possession of our property and the free and public exercise of the Roman Catholic religion, we desire to continue, to the utmost of our power, to be faithful and dutiful..."

Letter from acting Nova Scotia Governor Charles Lawrence to Lt.-Col. John Winslow at Grand-Pré and Capt. Alexander Murray at Pisiquid, August 1755.

"Having in my Letter of the 31st of July Last Acquainted Captain Murray with the reasons which Induced His Majesty's Council to Come to the Resolution of Sending Away the French Inhabitants and Clearing the Whole Country of Such Bad Subjects...it only Remains for Me to Give you Necessary Orders and Instructions for Puting in Practice What has Ben So Solemnly Determined.

"That the Inhabitants May Not have it in their Power to return to this Province, Nor to Join in Strengthening the French of Canada or Louisbourge, it is Resolved that they shall be Dispersed Among His Majesty's Colonies Upon the Continent of America.

"For this purpose Transports are Sent Up the Bay to Ship of those at Chignecto And Colonel Monckton will Order those he Cannot fill their unto Mines Bason to Carry oft Some part of the Inhabitants of these Districts; you Will have Vessels Also from Boston to transport one Thousand Persons Reckoning Two Persons to a Ton."

expressed in the Acadians' petition. The British administration in Halifax, like other contemporary governments, was looking for obedient subjects.

On June 24, eight days after the French commander at Beauséjour surrendered to the British force on June 16, forty-four Acadians of Les Mines, Pisiquid, and River Canard sent a second petition to acting governor Charles Lawrence. This time they asked for forgiveness if anything in the first petition showed a lack of respect. (One assumes that they had learned that the first petition was not well received by the authorities.) The Acadians asked for the opportunity to explain their reasoning behind their petition to Lawrence and the Council.

A New MAP of
NOVA SCOTIA
with its Boundaries,
according to M. D'Anvile.
Engraved by
T. Jefferys Geographer to
His Royal Highness the
PRINCE of WALES.

To the
Right Hon. the
Lords Commissioners for
Trade and Plantations,
This PLATE
is most humbly presented
by your Lordships
Most Obedient and Devoted
humble Servant
T. Jefferys.

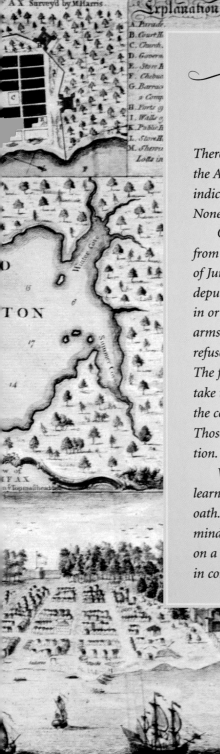

First Set of Deputies Goes to Halifax

There are no documents that provide insight into the thoughts and moods of the Acadian deputies as they travelled to Halifax. Nor is there any evidence to indicate how they coped with what happened to them after they arrived. Nonetheless, it is safe to assume that the experience was tense and worrisome.

On July 3, the Nova Scotia Council interrogated the Acadian deputies from Les Mines and Pisiquid who had come to Halifax to explain the petitions of June 10 and 24. At the end of the session, the council demanded the deputies take the standard oath of loyalty. The British officials had no interest in or sympathy for any oath that would exempt the Acadians from bearing arms or otherwise preserve their neutrality. The Acadian representatives refused to swear the oath and were given the night to think over their decision. The following day, July 4, the Acadian deputies reaffirmed their decision not to take the oath without consulting their home communities. With that answer, the council decided to have new deputies selected in Les Mines and Pisiquid. Those representatives were to come to Halifax to answer the same oath question. Should they refuse, it was resolved, they were to be deported.

When the deputies in Halifax who had already refused to take the oath learned the consequences of their decision, they offered to take the standard oath. The Nova Scotia Council, however, would not let them change their mind. The British officials reasoned that a promise of allegiance must be based on a true commitment, not a fear of consequences. The deputies were placed in confinement on Georges Island in Halifax harbour.

A view of Halifax—the primary British stronghold in the region—only a few years before the Acadian deputies arrived there in July 1755. All deputies who came to Halifax for the two meetings of July 1755 ended up being imprisoned on Georges Island and eventually deported.

MORE PETITIONS, ANOTHER TRIP TO HALIFAX

On Sunday, July 13, 207 inhabitants of the Acadian community in the Annapolis region assembled to draw up their petition to acting governor Lawrence and the Nova Scotia Council. They unanimously consented to deliver their firearms to Maj. Handfield, the British commander at Annapolis Royal. Back in Halifax on July 14, the Nova Scotia Council invited the two British admirals who were in port, Edward Boscawen and Savage Mostyn, to attend the next meeting of the council. At that upcoming meeting, the admirals were informed, the "Security of the Province" was to be discussed.

Brook Watson, who took part in the expedition that captured the French fort at Beauséjour in 1755 and who later became a prominent political agent and merchant, would recall in 1791 that Adm. Boscawen played a determining role, along with Lawrence, in the decision to send "all Acadians out of the country." That opinion was of course authored decades after the event. The minutes of the Nova Scotia Council record simply that, on July 15, Adm. Boscawen and Vice-Adm. Mostyn attended the council meeting and "gave it as their opinion that it was now the properest Time to oblige the said Inhabitants to take the Oath of Allegiance to His Majesty or to quit the Country." Given the senior rank of the two admirals, their opinions likely carried weight with Lawrence and the rest of the council.

"…gave it as their opinion that it was now the properest Time to oblige the said Inhabitants to take the Oath of Allegiance to His Majesty or to quit the Country."

On July 22, two new petitions were composed in different Acadian communities. One was drawn up on behalf of 203 inhabitants of Les Mines, Canard River, and neighbouring villages. The 103 inhabitants of Pisiquid signed the other. The second document began by making reference to the oath of fidelity taken in 1729–30 when Richard Philipps was Nova Scotia's governor. That was back when the British capital had still been at Annapolis Royal. The petition explained that they had sworn a conditional oath "with all the circumstances and reservation granted to us." The petition further stated that the Acadians had "observed" that allegiance "as far as possible." Accordingly, "we are all resolved, with one consent and voice, to take no other oath. We hope, Sir, that you will have the kindness to listen to our just reasons; and, in consequence, we all, with a unanimous voice, beg his honor to set at liberty our people who have been detained at Halifax for some time, not even knowing their situation, which appears to us deplorable."

The Acadian petitions again used forceful language. The reactions that Lawrence and the other members of the Nova Scotia Council had when they read or heard the Acadians' choice of words can be imagined, but is not recorded. It was not likely sympathetic.

On July 25, the July 13 petition from the Annapolis region was read and discussed by the Nova Scotia Council. The deputies from Annapolis who were present were asked to take the oath. They refused, stating they preferred to "quit their Lands." The council gave them nearly 72 hours to reconsider. On Monday, July 28, at 10:00 A.M., the council was to receive their final answer.

On July 28, 1755, the council discussed the petition from the inhabitants of Pisiquid, and the one from Les Mines, Canard River, and nearby villages. The Acadian deputies detained in Halifax over the weekend were brought in to give their definitive answers to the oath question. The deputies unanimously refused to take the standard oath. Moreover, they expressed their willingness to relocate if allowed to choose where and when they could go. How much anguish the Acadian deputies went through over the weekend in reaching that consensus will never be known. The council then authorized a wholesale deportation of all Acadians.

The consequences of the July 28 decision would leave no Acadian individual or family untouched. Regardless of his or her individual positions on the imperial questions of the day—neutral, pro-French or pro-British—everyone's life would be completely overwhelmed in the weeks ahead. The Nova Scotia Council unanimously determined that neutrality was no longer an option. Thirteen days earlier, on July 15, the council had given it as their collective opinion that "it is now the Properest Time to oblige the said inhabitants to take the Oath of Allegiance to His Majesty or

Nova Scotia
~ Council ~

The members of the Nova Scotia Council during this series of fateful meetings were:

- **Charles Lawrence** (c. 1709-60)
  English-born military officer and acting governor of Nova Scotia
- **Benjamin Green** (1713-72)
  Massachusetts-born merchant and office-holder
- **John Collier** (?-1769)
  English-born retired army officer
- **William Cotterell**
  (dates and details unknown)
- **John Rous** (c. 1700-60)
  New England naval and privateer captain
- **Jonathan Belcher** (1710-76)
  Boston-born, Harvard- and Cambridge-educated lawyer and Chief Justice of Nova Scotia

to quit the Country." With the standard oath clearly rejected, the Deportation decision went ahead. Acting governor Charles Lawrence would soon write that the resolution was one of "Sending Away the French Inhabitants and Clearing the Whole Country of Such Bad Subjects." The colonial authorities initially attempted to prepare carefully for the evacuation, but, in the end, it was poorly planned and brutally implemented.

PLANS AND ACTIONS, AUGUST 1755

The implementation of the Nova Scotia Council's policy of forcible removal of the Acadians began at Fort Cumberland (as the fort at Beauséjour had been renamed) on August 11. A summons went out for Acadian males in the Chignecto area to come to the fort. The cut-off age is not known, but at Grand-Pré, a month later, men and boys aged ten and over were asked to attend an announcement. Two hundred and fifty males came into Fort Cumberland on August 11, 1755. They were all detained, then transferred to Fort Lawrence, atop the facing ridge, where they were imprisoned. One of the officers who witnessed the initial round-up in the Chignecto area was Lt.-Col. John Winslow, a Massachusetts officer who was second in command to Lt.-Col. Monckton on the expedition to take the forts at Beauséjour and Gaspareau. Winslow would soon be at Grand-Pré, implementing essentially the same policy.

A small but significant number of Acadians, especially in the Petitcoudiac, Shepody, and Memramcook areas, took up arms and began to resist the New England and British soldiers.

In the days and weeks that followed the August 11 imprisonment of Acadian males at Fort Cumberland, attempts were made to round up all Acadians in the Chignecto region and in the Cobequid district. The New England soldiers burned the buildings in the abandoned villages and in those areas where they rounded up people. Some Acadians, including nearly all in the Cobequid district, escaped before the soldiers arrived. The vast majority fled to Île Saint-Jean, which would remain a French colony until the late summer of 1758. A small but significant number of Acadians, especially in the Petitcoudiac, Shepody, and Memramcook areas, took up arms and began to resist the New England and British soldiers.

On the very same day that 250 Acadian males were imprisoned at Fort Cumberland, acting governor Charles Lawrence wrote a series of letters. One letter was composed for each Lt.-Col. Winslow and Capt. Alexander Murray, who were instructed to oversee deportations in the Grand-Pré and Pisiquid regions. As of that date, Lawrence expected that Acadians would be shipped off in the following manner: 500 to North Carolina, 1,000 to Virginia, and 500 to Maryland. (The numbers and destinations would change later.) Also on August 11, Lawrence wrote a common letter to each of the governors of the Anglo-American colonies, explaining what had happened and why. Those letters were not sent right away—they would go with the captains of the ships transporting the deported Acadians when they left Nova Scotia waters. Thus the governors of the destination colonies would know nothing about the Deportation until the first Acadians arrived. There would be no preparations as to how to accommodate them or what to do with them.

...the governors of the destination colonies would know nothing about the Deportation until the first Acadians arrived. There would be no preparations as to how to accommodate them or what to do with them.

Lawrence envisioned the Deportation as the military operation that it was. He planned to make full use of the approximately 2,000 New England and 300 British soldiers that had come to the colony for the capture of the fort at Beauséjour, and that were now available for other purposes.

The operation began with the Acadians in the Chignecto area. On August 13, two days after the Acadian men of the Chignecto region were induced to enter Fort Cumberland where they were arrested, Lt.-Col. John Winslow of the Massachusetts regiment received orders to proceed to Pisiquid. The British base at Pisiquid was Fort Edward, which stood on a hill overlooking the sizeable Acadian community and the two rivers that provided the easiest transportation links in the district. On August 16, Winslow set sail from the Chignecto region for Pisiquid with about 300 soldiers. The contingent arrived there the next day. Winslow went immediately to Fort Edward to see the British officer in charge, Capt. Alexander Murray. Winslow opened the orders from Lawrence and learned that his new task was to oversee the "Transportation of the Inhabitants of the Districts of Minas, Piziquid, River of Canard, Cobequid & c out of the province of Nova Scotia."

Winslow would soon write, in a letter to Gov. Shirley of Massachusetts, that it was going to be "a Disagreable Business to remove People from their Antient Habitations, which, in this part of the Countrey, are Verry Valuable." Disagreeable or not, Winslow set about to carry out his orders. On the next tide, he proceeded by ship to Grand-Pré. Capt. Murray remained at Fort Edward where he would be the officer responsible for the removal of the Acadians from Pisiquid and the surrounding area. Over the next few months, as events developed, Winslow and Murray would be in frequent contact over how best to assist each other in executing their orders.

When Winslow arrived in Grand-Pré on August 19, 1755, it was not his first time there. In the 1740s, he had been an officer in the Philipps

Regiment in the garrison at Annapolis Royal, and he had been to Grand-Pré at least once. This time, however, the stakes were completely different.

Lt.-Col. Winslow's first action at Grand-Pré was to establish a secure base of operations for his soldiers. He knew what lay ahead and he realized that his 300-man force was greatly outnumbered by the Acadian population in the area, which numbered close to 2,200. Of course, Winslow's soldiers had weapons and the Acadians did not. Moreover, the New England troops were battle-hardened from the siege at Beauséjour, while the local Acadians were fundamentally an agricultural population. Nonetheless, the Massachusetts commander worried greatly about being outnumbered and he wanted to place his contingent in a strong position to reduce the risk of an uprising or revolt.

To give himself a stronghold in the centre of Grand-Pré, Winslow selected the area around the parish church, Saint-Charles-des-Mines. His soldiers erected a palisade around the priest's house, the church, and the cemetery. The troops pitched their tents within that enclosed area and Winslow occupied the priest's home. So as not to upset the Acadians unnecessarily, Winslow informed community leaders that they should remove the sacred objects from the church prior their occupancy.

Did the Acadians at this point begin to suspect that something serious was about to happen? There are no sources to suggest the thoughts and emotions of the people of Grand-Pré as they watched the soldiers go about their business. In his journal, Winslow wrote nothing that indicates the Acadians were showing signs of panic or even apprehension. The most likely explanation is that the men, women, and children of the community thought they were seeing the establishment of a temporary British base. Back in the winter of 1746–47, New England troops had made a camp at Grand-Pré, and there was subsequently a manned post in the community between 1749 and 1754, at what was called the Vieux Logis. Thus it may not have seemed at all unusual that there were once again British and New England soldiers at Grand-Pré.

Not far away in Pisiquid, Capt. Murray at Fort Edward assessed the situation in much the same way as Winslow. Murray reported the following: "I was out yesterday at the Villages. All the People were [quiet] and very Busy at their Harvest." On the surface at least, the Acadians were taking the arrival of the troops and the construction of a palisaded stronghold at Grand-Pré in their stride. Among themselves, in private conversations, perhaps there were those who voiced their fears and suspicions.

As August came to a close and September began, the Acadians turned their attention to the work at hand—the harvest. Though there had been harvests in many different conditions over the preceding seventy-five years, that of 1755 would be unlike any seen before.

Re-creation of Acadians signing an oath in 1730, which exempted them from bearing arms during conflicts. The local governor, however, did not inform his superiors in London of this compromise—they would have rejected it. In subsequent years, the Acadians consistently referred to this oath, steadfastly defending their position of neutrality and their refusal to sign another oath; particularly in 1755.

CHAPTER THREE

THE TRAGEDY UNFOLDS

On September 4, 1755, Lt.-Col. John Winslow issued what he described as a "Citation" to the Acadian inhabitants of Grand-Pré. The message would have been read aloud and it may have been posted as well. The core of the citation was that all men and boys aged ten and older were to come to the parish church at three o'clock in the afternoon on the following day to hear an important announcement. A similar ploy was used by Capt. Murray to call Acadian males in the Pisiquid region to Fort Edward on the same day. Essentially the same approach had been adopted a month earlier in the Chignecto region, to entice males there into what the Acadians knew as the fort at Beauséjour, which the British called Fort Cumberland.

THE ANNOUNCEMENT

On September 5, 418 Acadian males in the Grand-Pré region proceeded, as requested, to the parish church of Saint-Charles-des-Mines. When they entered the church they saw a table in the centre of the church, and a number of Winslow's officers nearby. Presumably there were armed soldiers as well. At three o'clock in the afternoon, Winslow had interpreters inform the assembled inhabitants that they and their families were to be deported, and "that your Lands and Tenements, Cattle of all Kinds and Live Stock of all Sortes are Forfitted to the Crown with all other your Effects Saving your money and Household Goods and you your Selves to be removed from this his Province."

Artist's interpretation of Acadian men and boys being marched off.

Winslow's order was as follows:

Gentlemen,

I have Received from his Excellency Governor Lawrence. The Kings Commission which I have in hand and by whose orders you are Convened togather to Manifest to you his Majesty's Final resolution to the French Inhabitants of this his Province of Nova Scotia. who for almost half a Century have had more Indulgence Granted them, then any of his Subjects in any part of his Dominions. what use you have made of them. you your Self Best Know.

The Part of Duty I am now upon is what thoth Necessary is Very Disagreeable to my natural make & Temper as I Know it Must be Grevious to you who are of the Same Specia.

But it is not my Business to annimedvert, but to obey Such orders as I receive and therefore without Hesitation Shall Deliver you his majesty's orders and Instructions vizt.

That your Lands and Tennements, Cattle of all Kinds and Live Stock of all Sortes are Forfitted to the Crown with all other your Effects Saving your money and Household Goods and you your Selves to be removed from this his Province.

Thus it is Preremtorily his Majesty's orders That the whole French Inhabitants of these Districts, be removed, and I am Throh his Majesty's Goodness Directed to allow you Liberty to Carry of your money and Household Goods as Many as you Can without Discomemoading the Vessels you Go in. I Shall do Every thing in my Power that all Those Goods be Secured to you and that you are Not Molested in Carrying of them of and also that whole Familys Shall go in the same Vessel. and make this remove which I am Sensable must give you a great Deal of Trouble as Easey as his Majesty's Service will admit and hope that in what Ever part of the world you may Fall you may be Faithful Subjects, a Peaseable & happy People.

I Must also Inform you That it is his Majesty's Pleasure that you remain in Security under the Inspection & Direction of the Troops that I have the Honr. to Command.

Winslow then declared them the "Kings Prisoners."

One imagines the varied reactions from the Acadians in the church. Some fell into stunned silence; others gave vent to their shock and anger. The only surviving eyewitness account, other than Winslow's, is that of Lt. Jeremiah Bancroft, a New England soldier. Bancroft recorded the look on their faces as being a mixture of "shame and confusion…together with anger." Bancroft added that the countenances of the Acadians were so altered it could not be expressed.

There was surely an incredible clamour from the men and boys in the church when they heard the interpreters speak Winslow's words. The Acadian women and children waiting beyond the palisaded enclosure, even perhaps those doing their chores some distance away, undoubtedly heard the cries. Perhaps the village came to a complete standstill as people wondered and worried about what was going on in their church.

Artists's interpretation of Lt.-Col. John Winslow reading the Deportation Order, September 5, 1755.

Grand Pre September the

The Names of the French Inhabitant belonging to Gran
Adjacent Confined by Lieut Colo Winslow within his
Citation on the 5th of September = past ——— 1755

Mens Names	Villages Names	Sons	Daughters
Jean Baptise Daigree	De Chaud Terlio		
Alexandre Landry	De Landry		
Antorne Vinsan	Do	1	
Olivir Aneoin	Do	1	1
5 Pierre Landry	De	4	4
Batiste Sapin	Do	4	2
Pierre Mellanson	Do	2	3
Jean a Pierre Landry	Do		
Charle Landry	Do	1	5
10 Claud Aneoine	De	1	
Antoine Landry apsen			
Jean Batistee Daigre	Des Terriote Do	3	4
Pierre Terriot	Do		
Janis Terrioh	Do	2	7
15 Charle A Claud Terrioh	Do	2	1
Cuprien Terrioh	Do	2	3
Michelle Richard	Do	4	4
Basil Richard	Do		
Pierre LeClane	Do		
20 Charle Daigre	Do		
Norez Landry	Des Landry		
Pierre Landry	Do		
Antoine Landry	Do		
Charle Daigre	Do		
25 Joseph Granger	Des Granger	1	5
Rener Granger	Do	2	5
Charle Granger	Do	6	5
Francois Granger	Do	1	
Jean Granger	Do	3	4

TO THE TRANSPORTS

Winslow feared there might be uprisings that his troops would not be able to handle. Therefore, on September 10, he ordered about 200 of the 418 men and boys imprisoned in the church to be separated from the rest and placed aboard five transport ships anchored in the basin. Seeing their fathers, sons, brothers, uncles, and other friends and relatives march off to the waiting ships surely convinced those not yet in custody that Lt.-Col. Winslow meant what he had announced on September 5. It was no bluff or scare tactic. Winslow recorded that as the men made their way from the parish church to the transport ships they "went off Praying, Singing, & Crying, being Met by the women & Children all the way…with Great Lamentations upon their knees praying."

Opening page of the lengthy list of Acadians living in Grand-Pré and nearby communities that was compiled in September 1755 at Winslow's request.

Map showing the Anglo-American colonies the Acadians from Grand-Pré and area were shipped to in late 1755

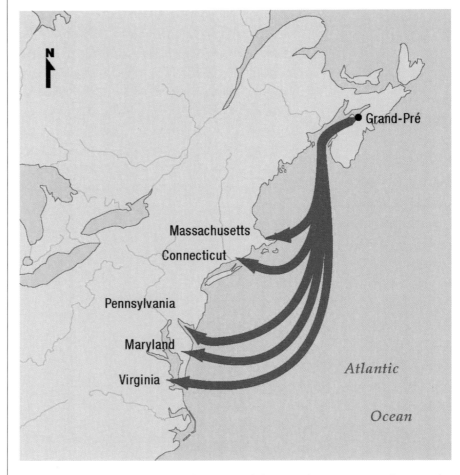

Massachusetts

Connecticut

Pennsylvania

Maryland

Virginia

Atlantic

Ocean

Grand-Pré

The subsequent removal of the rest of the population at Grand-Pré and the neighbouring villages did not proceed quickly or smoothly. Winslow had to cope with a shortage of transport ships and a lack of sufficient provisions. Foodstuffs in large quantities were needed to sustain the approximately 2,200 people who were going to be sent to the Anglo-American colonies. For the men and boys already rounded up, it meant six more weeks of imprisonment, either in the church of Saint-Charles-des-Mines or on board the transport ships anchored in the Minas Basin. The women and children still in the family homes lived in anguish as they worried about their loved ones.

The wholesale embarkation at Grand-Pré began on October 8. Winslow recorded that the inhabitants left "unwillingly, the women in Great Distress Carrying off Their Children in their Arms, Others Carrying their Decrepit Parents in their Carts and all their Goods moving in Great Confusion and appeared a scene of Woe and Distress." The commanding officer from Massachusetts gave orders that the families were to be kept together. Yet in the chaos and hurry this was not always possible. Moreover, for Acadians a family usually included more than a mother, father, and children. There were also grandparents, in-laws, aunts, uncles, cousins, nephews, and nieces. As a result, relatives, friends, and neighbours of a lifetime were sometimes separated, never to see each other again.

From October 19 to 21, more families from the outlying communities were assembled at Budrot Point, located between the Rivers Canard and Habitant. Approximately 600 inhabitants, from 98 families, were brought to Grand-Pré. While they awaited the arrival of the transport ships, they were lodged in the recently vacated homes near Winslow's camp.

By late October 1755, over 1,500 Acadian men, women, and children—with children more numerous than adults—from Grand-Pré and nearby villages had been herded onto the transport ships. The convoy then sailed out of the Minas Basin bound for Pennsylvania, Virginia, Maryland, Connecticut, and Massachusetts. At the same time, transport ships carrying over 1,000 Acadian deportees from the Pisiquid area also sailed south to the Anglo-American colonies.

To prevent Acadians from ever returning to their homes, Winslow and Murray destroyed what they called the "Out Villages" in their districts. Smoke hung over the marshlands for days as soldiers set fire to hundreds of buildings. In the region close to Grand-Pré, some 700 houses, barns, and other structures were destroyed. Grand-Pré itself was initially spared because it was the site of Winslow's headquarters, and the temporary holding spot for the Acadians from Budrot Point. There is no document that states that the village of Grand-Pré was destroyed. That is because Winslow left the area before the last troops withdrew, and it is his journal that provides details. Certainly, the plan had been to destroy the village once the soldiers no longer needed it. That probably happened in late December 1755. Until then, the approximately 600 Acadians brought from Budrot Point were held in the houses. They were sent into exile in mid- to late December—350 on December 13 and the remainder a week later, where-upon Capt. Osgood wrote to Winslow that "This serves to Inform you that the French which you left under my Care are all removed. The last of them Sailed this afternoon [December 20]."

In total, approximately 2,200 Acadians were deported from Grand-Pré and the surrounding area. That figure makes up roughly one third of the more than 6,000 Acadians who were deported from Nova Scotia in 1755.

~ Last Look ~

Artist's interpretation of what it may have been like aboard one of the transports as the Acadians sailed out of the Minas Basin. Most would never again see the familiar landmark of Cape Blomidon. The majority of the Acadians who were deported in 1755 never returned to the Maritimes. Of those who did, only a small percentage ever came back to where their villages had once stood. When they did, they discovered that the lands had been granted to "Planters" from New England.

DEADLY VOYAGES

The children, women, and men of Grand-Pré and nearby villages were crammed onto transport ships that would carry them to various Anglo-American colonies. It is easy to write that the deportees were filled with worry, heartbreak, and a sense of loss. Such words, however, are unlikely to convey the anguish the Acadians felt as they were forced onto ships for destinations that were unfamiliar and maybe even unknown. After all, the land they were being forced to leave was not just home; it was land that they or their forebears had created, reclaiming it from the sea over generations. After 75 years of Acadian occupation, the lands at Grand-Pré and area were deserted. The area ceased to know the Acadians as a united people.

Aboard the transports, the deportees endured wretched conditions of all sorts: storms, food shortages, foul drinking water, contagious diseases, and squalor. As many as one third of the Acadians may have died of contagious diseases, either at sea or shortly after their arrival in the Anglo-American colonies.

The ships sailed into seaports with no advance notice. Lawrence's letters to each of the Anglo-American governors, explaining what happened, arrived with the Acadians. The Anglo-American colonists were far from pleased to see the ships with their human cargoes. They viewed the deportees as unwanted interlopers. For starters, there was the matter of the sicknesses they were carrying. No one wanted to admit people who were sick and dying. Then again, even if the Acadians had been healthy, the English-speaking Protestant populations were fearful of admitting a large number of French-speaking Roman Catholics into their midst. Given that war with the French was expected to be declared soon, they thought accepting them was a dangerous and unwise action.

The hostility of the Anglo-Americans toward the Acadians showed itself in different ways. Virginia refused its complement. Governor Dinwiddie of Virginia reflected the prejudices of the period when he wrote that the "French Neutrals…[are]bigotted Papists, lazy and contentious." Those deportees disembarked, but then in May 1756 they were sent to England, where many would die before the survivors were finally accepted by France. The other Anglo-American colonies to which the Acadians were

As many as one third of the Acadians may have died of contagious diseases, either at sea or shortly after their arrival in the Anglo-American colonies.

Once apprehended, they were generally used as cheap, skilled labour, particularly in maintaining and repairing the dykes in the area.

sent did accept, reluctantly, their contingents, yet the deportees would remain outsiders in the communities where they settled.

Back in the Les Mines area, some Acadians did manage to evade the initial round-up for deportation by hiding in the forests. Oral traditions among the Mi'kmaq talk of how their ancestors helped the Acadians. Most Acadians, however, eventually surrendered or were captured. Fort Edward was the place of imprisonment for those rounded up in the Les Mines area and elsewhere. Fort Cumberland and Fort Lawrence played the same role in the Chignecto area. Many prisoners came from places of refuge in what is now New Brunswick. Once apprehended, they were generally used as cheap, skilled labour, particularly in maintaining and repairing the dykes in the area. Beginning in 1760, settlers known as Planters from New England began taking over the fertile farmlands from which the Acadians had been removed. The Planters needed advice and assistance from the Acadians on how to maintain the old dykes, and how to construct new ones.

A Plea for Help

Province of the Massachusetts Bay

To His Excellency Spensor Phips Esq. Lieutenant Governor of Said Province and to the Honourable Council of the same

The humble Petition of Augustin Hebert Most Humbly sheweth

That your Petitioner now residing at Water town has been most inhumanly us'd of late by Capt. Couligas who has forced from him one of his Children while your Petitioner maintained him by his own Industry, and not satisfied with that, has so beat your distressed Petitioner that he was scarce able to walk about for a fortnight all which the subscribers can certifie, it is a very hard trial for a Man to see his Child ravished away from him and to be so desparately Beat and his Wife ill us'd withal, yet relying on your Justice and equity submit to your wise consideration hoping you will redress and rectofy this grievance and Your Petitioner as in duty Bound shall over Pray.

> *Signum*
> *Augustin x Hebert*

Witness to this Grievance
> *Signum*
>> *Paul x Braux*
> *Signum*
>> *Jean x Landry*
>> *Chas. x Hebert*
>> *Jaq. x Hebert*
>> *Pierre x Hebert*
>> *Augustin x Hebert*
>> *Antoine x Hebert*
>> *Olivier o Hebert*
>> *Joseph x Hebert*
>> *Fra. x Landry*

October 7th 1756

Augustin Hebert pleads for justice in a letter after the abduction of one of his children. Ten witnesses countersign his plea.

EIGHT LONG YEARS

What occurred at Grand-Pré in 1755 has long been the symbol of the Deportation, yet essentially the same processes of round-ups, embarkations, and scorched-earth destruction took place at various locations throughout the region, and continued sporadically until 1762. Many of the Acadians who escaped the deportations in 1755—such as the entire village of Cobequid, where everyone vanished before the New England soldiers arrived—made their way to the French colony of Île Saint-Jean. In 1758, the British would take over Île Saint-Jean and deport about 3,100 Acadians and French to France. In the period from 1755 to 1758, some Acadians who avoided the forced removals fled to the Miramichi district of what is now northern New Brunswick. There, they organized a resistance against those who would imprison and deport them. Many of those who escaped to the woods, with assistance from some Mi'kmaq and Wolastoqiyik (Maliseet), suffered from extreme cold, exhaustion, and starvation. Some were reduced to eating the soles of their shoes or rotten animal carcasses. Many refugees eventually died. The survivors fled to Canada (today's Quebec), were imprisoned in British forts in Nova Scotia and what is now New Brunswick, were used as cheap labour, or were deported.

SURVIVAL AND ADAPTATION

Back in July 1755, when the Nova Scotia Council debated whether or not to implement a wholesale deportation policy for the Acadians, the location initially mentioned as a destination was France or the French colonies. In the end, however, they worried such a population increase would strengthen their

enemy. Instead, they chose the Anglo-American colonies to the south. The officials did not use terms like assimilation, yet that is clearly what they wanted.

What the members of the Nova Scotia Council, and others who supported the policy, failed to understand or appreciate was the Acadians' will to survive and their unshakeable desire to retain their ways and identity. Such strength came from years of self-reliance and successful struggle against forces that often threatened their way of life. A large number of deportees sent to the Anglo-American colonies along the Atlantic seaboard, or to British and French ports, would later undertake journeys that took them to Louisiana, the West Indies, France, Quebec, and back to the Maritimes. Wherever they found themselves, they set about beginning again.

Footsore and half-clad, many dispossessed Acadians in the Anglo-American colonies searched for lost family members and friends. They endured extreme poverty and a series of hardships. And they anguished at seeing their children used as cheap labour and as objects of public humiliation.

Admittedly, some Acadians were so shattered by what they experienced in 1755 and subsequent years that they lost their sense of identity as Acadians. Willingly or unwillingly, they were absorbed into the mainstream population of the Anglo-American colonies, and elsewhere, to which they were sent.

Sizeable numbers of Acadians eventually made their way to Canada or Louisiana. As French colonies between 1755 and 1763, neither had been a territory to which the British wanted to send Acadians. After 1763, however, the treaty that ended the Seven Years' War made Louisiana a Spanish colony, while Canada became Quebec, a French-speaking British colony. In both places, Roman Catholicism was the official religion, creating environments appealing to many Acadians.

A significant minority of Acadians in the Anglo-American colonies and elsewhere did not yield to the pressures of assimilation. Nor did they choose to live in surroundings and a climate drastically different from what they had once known. For them, the desire both to maintain a distinctive identity and to find a place where they could live as they chose was strong. For that segment of Acadian deportees, there would be long years of wandering and migration that ultimately led many back to Canada's Maritime Provinces.

> *In 1764, the Acadians received permission to resettle in their former homeland of Nova Scotia, provided they swore allegiance to the monarch of Great Britain.*

For those who wanted to return to Grand-Pré, Pisiquid, Cobequid, and other areas devastated in 1755, the Acadie they had known no longer existed. New England Planters now occupied most of their former farming areas.

In 1764, the Acadians received permission to resettle in their former homeland of Nova Scotia, provided they swore allegiance to the monarch of Great Britain. Slowly but persistently, small groups began to return. Beginning the long trek home, they made their way mainly by boat from as far away as South Carolina and Georgia. When they discovered, or heard, that newcomers from New England occupied most of their former areas, the Acadians had no choice but to settle elsewhere. They were joined by Acadians finally released from imprisonment in the region, and those who had been in hiding. Most ended up in areas that had little or no agricultural potential in what are now Nova Scotia, New Brunswick, Prince Edward Island, and Quebec. They found other ways to make a living. Most turned to the sea and to the forest for new livelihoods.

Buffeted for over a generation, the Acadians finally established several new Acadies, since the communities were dispersed over much of what are now the Maritime Provinces and in Quebec. The new Acadian society, spread out as it was and made up of many shattered families, was less cohesive than the original. Nonetheless, despite the hardships the Acadians survived and rebuilt their world. Today, there are millions of descendants around the world. The five main concentrations are in the Atlantic region, Quebec, Louisiana, New England, and France.

THE CREATION OF A NATIONAL HISTORIC SITE

*A*mong the many locations that witnessed the forcible removal of Acadians between 1755 and 1762, Grand-Pré emerged as the site most strongly identified with the tragedy of the *Grand Dérangement*.

There are two main reasons for Grand-Pré's pre-eminence. The first is that Lt.-Col. John Winslow, the Massachusetts officer in charge of deporting Acadians from the Les Mines area, kept a detailed journal of what happened. Nothing comparable exists for any other Acadian community. The second reason is that Henry Wadsworth Longfellow selected Grand-Pré as the setting for the first half of his poem *Evangeline, A Tale of Acadie*, published in 1847. Longfellow may not have read Winslow's journal, but the renowned American poet acknowledged that he relied on Thomas Chandler Haliburton's history of Nova Scotia, published in 1827, which did make great use of Winslow's account. From the time of its publication, *Evangeline* was a literary sensation. Millions of readers, first in the United States and eventually around the world, came to know the tragic love story. In the course of its first hundred years, *Evangeline* witnessed at least 270 editions and 130 translations. The success of the poem, which came out in an illustrated edition beginning in 1850, made Grand-Pré the most famous of all pre-Deportation sites.

For the Acadians, the tragedy and trauma that they or their ancestors lived through remained an oral history tradition until Longfellow produced his poetic version of the experience. Mixing fact with fiction in a romantic writing style, *Evangeline* drew attention to and generated sympathy for Acadian history and culture. Longfellow's fictional characters, especially his heroine, became real for many readers.

The poem also had an impact on the Acadians' sense of their own worth. It contributed immeasurably to the growing spirit of Acadian

John Frederic Herbin

nationalism in the later 1800s. As the nineteenth century wore on, there developed a strong sense of Acadian identity. Their determination to survive as a people, a distinct people with a unique history, was re-awakened.

While Longfellow's poem and Winslow's journal are central to the history of Grand-Pré, it was John Frederic Herbin who in the early twentieth century had the vision that ensured the preservation of the actual grounds. Herbin, whose mother was an Acadian, led a campaign to have the site of Grand-Pré preserved as a memorial.

Early in the twentieth century, Herbin wrote: "Grand-Pré is the home of Longfellow's 'Evangeline,' and a stone memorial there would be fitting to perpetuate the name of the poet….Imperishable marble should mark the place, and tell its history to many persons who come every year [to visit]….A fund is now being raised for the purpose of making of this ground an Acadian and Longfellow Memorial Park." For many Acadians, a visit to Grand-Pré was, and still is, akin to a pilgrimage.

Herbin purchased the land believed to be the site of the parish church and cemetery of Saint-Charles-des-Mines in 1907. The following year the Nova Scotia legislature passed an act to incorporate the "Trustees of Grand Pré Historic Grounds." Herbin erected a stone cross on the site to mark the cemetery, using stones from the remains of what he believed were Acadian foundations. In 1917, he and the trustees sold the property to the Dominion Atlantic Railway (DAR) on condition that the church site be deeded to the Acadian people, so that they could erect a memorial to their ancestors. The DAR assumed responsibility for the property and landscaped the grounds. In 1920, the railway company unveiled a bronze statue of Evangeline, the work of Quebec sculptor Henri Hébert, who produced a variation on an earlier design of his father, sculptor Louis-Philippe Hébert.

Commemorative stamp of Grand-Pré, 1930

The Dominion Atlantic Railway used the association of Grand-Pré with Longfellow's *Evangeline* to promote the railway. Similarly, Nova Scotia Tourism undertook promotions using the Evangeline theme. The commercialization of Evangeline was off and running. Examples of Evangeline as promoter included the "Evangeline Trail," "Land of Evangeline," soft drinks, car dealerships, chocolates, and a newspaper.

Unveiling of Henri Hébert's statue of Evangeline, July 29, 1920

DAR "Land of Evangeline" logo

Despite the commercial aspects, the symbolic figure of Evangeline remains a powerful icon of the Deportation, connecting Longfellow's legacy to the Acadian people and to the history of Grand-Pré National Historic Site of Canada.

At a special ceremony at Grand-Pré during the 1921 Acadian National Convention, the Société mutuelle de l'Assomption took official possession of the church site. The following year the Société built the Memorial Church. Acadians and their friends and supporters from throughout North America donated the required funds. The erection of the church reflected the spirit of nationalism and the renaissance of Acadians.

Grand-Pré continued as an important focus of the Acadian renaissance throughout the decades that followed. A statue of the Acadian patron saint, Notre-Dame de l'Assomption, was placed within the church, as was an Acadian flag. The interior of the Memorial Church was completed in 1930.

One of the most poignant symbols commemorating the Deportation is the lone iron cross that is located about two kilometers from the Memorial

Voyage du Devoir en ACADIE, 1924
8 HORTON LANDING — Bénédiction de la Croix commémorative
de l'embarquement des déportés

Above: Group from Louisiana at Grand-Pré, 1936

Opposite: Dedication of the Embarkation Cross, 1924

Below: Dedication of the Memorial Church at Grand-Pré, August 18, 1922

Church. The cross stands solemnly in the marshlands formerly dyked and farmed by the Acadians. The cross marks what in the mid-1920s was believed to be the spot where the Acadians from the Grand-Pré area were embarked during the Deportation. Researchers now believe that the actual embarkation spot was approximately one kilometre closer to the basin.

In August 1955, thousands of Acadians from across North America gathered at Grand-Pré Park to mark the 200th anniversary of the Deportation. A bust of Longfellow, a gift from the Government of Nova Scotia, was unveiled during the event.

The Government of Canada acquired Grand Pré Memorial Park in 1957, and declared it a national historic site in 1961. The 1956 agreement between the federal government and the Société Nationale l'Assomption, acting on behalf of the Acadian people, acknowledged that "…Grand Pré Park is considered the most important Historic Site by the Acadian people…it recalls their saddest and most heroic moments and…must remain for future generations the example of courageous people whose culture and actions shall enrich more and more the Canadian nation."

FURTHER READING

Arsenault, Georges. *The Island Acadians,* 1720–1980. Translated by Sally Ross. Charlottetown: Ragweed Press, 1989.

Basque, Maurice. *Des hommes de pouvoir* : *Histoire d'Otho Robichaud et de sa famille, notables acadiens de Port-Royal et de Néguac.* Néguac: Société historique de Néguac, 1996.

Bertrand, Gabriel. "La culture des marais endigués et le développement de la solidarité militante en Acadie entre 1710 et 1755," *Cahiers de la Société historique acadienne* 24, no. 4 : 238–49.

Brebner, John Bartlet. *New England's Outpost: Acadia before the Conquest of Canada.* New York: Columbia University Press, 1927.

Brun, Régis. *Les Acadiens avant 1755 : essai.* Moncton: Régis Brun, 2003.

Buckner, Phillip A., and John G. Reid, eds. *The Atlantic Region to Confederation: A History.* Toronto: University of Toronto Press, 1994.

Butzer, Karl W. "French Wetland Agriculture in Atlantic Canada and Its European Roots: Different Avenues to Historical Diffusion," *Annals of the Association of American Geographers* 92, no. 3 (September 2002): 452–70.

Chevrier, Cécile. *Acadie : Esquisses d'un parcours / Sketches of a journey.* Dieppe, N.-B.: La Société Nationale de l'Acadie, 1994.

Clark, Andrew Hill. Acadia: *The Geography of Early Nova Scotia to 1760.* Madison: University of Wisconsin Press, 1968.

Conrad, Margaret, Alvin Finkel, and Cornelius Jaenen. *History of the Canadian Peoples. Vol. 1, Beginnings to 1867.* Toronto: Copp Clark Pitman, 1993.

Conrad, Margaret, ed. *Looking into Acadie: Three Illustrated Studies.* Halifax: Nova Scotia Museum, Curatorial Report No. 87, n.d.

Cormier, Yves. *Les Aboiteaux en Acadie, hier et aujourd'hui.* Moncton: Chaire d'études acadiennes, 1990.

Daigle, Jean, ed. *Acadia of the Maritimes: Thematic Studies From the Beginning to the Present.* Moncton: Chaire d'études acadiennes, 1995.

Daigle, Jean, and Robert LeBlanc. "Acadian Deportation and Return." *Historical Atlas of Canada. Vol I, From the Beginning to 1800,* edited by R. Cole Harris and Geoffrey J. Matthews. Toronto: University of Toronto Press, 1987, pl. 30.

Dawson, Joan. *The Mapmaker's Eye: Nova Scotia Through Early Maps.* Halifax: Nimbus Publishing and the Nova Scotia Museum, 1988.

Doucet, Clive. *Notes from Exile: On Being Acadian.* Toronto: McClelland and Stewart, 1999.

Dunn, Brenda. *The Acadians of Minas.* Ottawa: Parks Canada, 1990.

Dunn, Brenda. *A History of Port-Royal / Annapolis Royal, 1605–1800.* Halifax: Nimbus Publishing, 2004.

Durand, Yves. "L'Acadie et les phénomènes de solidarité et de fidelité au XVIIIe siècle," *Études canadiennes/Canadian Studies* 13 (1982) : 81–84.

Griffiths, Naomi E. S. *The Contexts of Acadian History, 1686–1784.* Montréal and Kingston: McGill-Queen's University Press, 1992.

Griffiths, N. E. S., comp. *The Acadian Deportation: Deliberate Perfidy or Cruel Necessity?* Toronto: Copp Clark, 1969.

Griffiths, Naomi. "The Golden Age: Acadian Life, 1713–1748," *Histoire sociale/Social History,* 17, no. 33 (May 1984): 21–34.

Johnston, A.J.B. "The Call of the Archetype and the Challenge of Acadian History," *French Colonial History,* Vol. 5 (2004): 63-92.

Johnston, A.J.B. "Borderland Worries: Loyalty Oaths in *Acadie* / Nova Scotia, 1654-1755," *French Colonial History,* Vol. 4 (2003): 31-48.

Landry, Nicolas, and Nicole Lang. *Histoire de l'Acadie.* Sillery, Quebec: Septentrion, c. 2001.

Laplante, Soeur Corinne. "Pourquoi les Acadiens sont-ils demeurés en Acadie? (1713–1720)." *Cahiers de la Société historique acadienne,* 21e Cahier, vol. 3, no. 1, (octobre–décembre 1968) : 4–17.

Lauvrière, Émile. *La Tragédie d'un peuple : Histoire du peuple acadien de ses origines à nos jours.* 2 vols. Paris : Éditions Bossard, 1922.

LeBlanc, Stéphane, et Jacques Vanderlinden. "Pauvre en France, riche en Acadie?," *Cahiers de la Société historique acadienne 29,* nos. 1 & 2 (mars–juin 1998): 10–33.

Le Blanc, Barbara. *Postcards from Acadie: Grand-Pré, Evangeline & the Acadian Identity.* Kentville, NS: Gaspereau Press, 2003.

Léger, Maurice A. "Les missionaires de l'ancienne Acadie (1604–1755)," *Cahiers de la Société historique acadienne* 28, nos. 2 & 3 (juin–septembre 1997): 63-97.

Moody, Barry. *The Acadians.* Toronto: Grolier, 1981.

Plank, Geoffrey. *An Unsettled Conquest: The British Campaign Against the Peoples of Acadia.* Philadelphia: University of Pennsylvania, 2000.

Reid, John G. *Six Crucial Decades: Times of Change in the History of the Maritimes.* Halifax: Nimbus Publishing, 1987.

Ross, Sally, and Alphonse Deveau. *The Acadians of Nova Scotia Past and Present.* Halifax: Nimbus Publishing, 1992.

Rouet, Damien. "L'Acadie, du comptoir à la colonie : Migration et colonisation du bassin des Mines (1680–1714)," *Cahiers de la Société historique acadienne* 29, nos. 1 & 2, (mars–juin 1998), 34-56.

Société Promotion Grand-Pré. "The Deportation of the Acadians," 2002.

Société Promotion Grand-Pré. "Dykes and Aboiteaux," 2003.

Taylor, M. Brook. "The Poetry and Prose of History: *Evangeline* and the Historians of Nova Scotia," *Journal of Canadian Studies* 23 (1988): 46–65.

Vanderlinden, Jacques. "Alliances entre familles acadiennes pendant la période française," *La Société historique acadienne—Les Cahiers* 27, nos. 2 et 3 (juin–septemebre 1996) : 125–148.

Viau, Robert. *Les visages d'Évangéline : Du poème au mythe.* Beauport, Quebec : MNH, 1998.

IMAGE SOURCES

p.viii   Italian map, 1566, National Archives of Canada

p. 3   Grand-Pré National Historic Site, François Gaudet

p. 4   Interpretation of Deportation, Artist Henri Beau, Musée acadien, Université de Moncton

p. 7   Jane E. Benham's engraving, Miriam Walls, Library of the Atlantic School of Theology

p. 8   Mi'kmaw family travelling by canoe, Mi'kmaq Association for Cultural Studies / Resources and Technology, Nova Scotia Department. of Education

p. 10   Detail of a map by Samuel de Champlain, *The Works of Samuel de Champlain*, Toronto, Champlain Society, 1922–1936

p. 11   Complex of buildings on St. Croix Island, National Archives of Canada

p. 13   Acadian couple in the 1640s, Artist Susan Tooke, Parks Canada

p. 14   Raising homes and barns, Artist Azor Vienneau, History Collection, Nova Scotia Museum

p. 15   Interpretation of Belleisle, Nova Scotia, 1730s, Artist Azor Vienneau, History Collection, Nova Scotia Museum

p. 16   Acadians were active traders, Artist Azor Vienneau, History Collection, Nova Scotia Museum

p. 18   Map highlighting Acadian settlements, Tim Daly, Parks Canada illustration

p. 19   Foster's illustration of Grand-Pré, 1850, Miriam Walls, Library of the Atlantic School of Theology

p. 21   Missionaries on their way to North America, Artist C.W. Jefferys, National Archives of Canada

p. 22   Buildings destroyed during the 1704 attack, Artist Claude Picard, Parks Canada

p. 24A   The "granary" of Acadia, Artist Azor Vienneau, History Collection, Nova Scotia Museum

p. 24B   Dyke construction, Artist Azor Vienneau, History Collection, Nova Scotia Museum

All other photographs are by François Gaudet, and appear courtesy of the Société Promotion Grand-Pré.